NEW ERA
BUSINESS ENGLISH

新时代
商务英语综合教程

学生用书

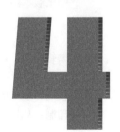
4

总 主 编　王立非

主 　 编　李新涛

副 主 编　王红雨　谢　娟

编 　 者　车　瑜　秦　燕

原著作者　〖英〗Ian Wood

　　　　　〖英〗Louise Pile

　　　　　〖英〗Sarah Curtis

清華大学出版社
北 京

Cengage Learning Asia Pte. Ltd.
151 Lorong Chuan, #02-08 New Tech Park, Singapore 556741
本书封面贴有 Cengage Learning 防伪标签，无标签者不得销售。

北京市版权局著作权合同登记号　图字：01–2018–0759

版权所有，侵权必究。举报：010-62782989，beiqinquan@tup.tsinghua.edu.cn。

图书在版编目（CIP）数据

新时代商务英语综合教程. 学生用书. 4 / 王立非总主编；李新涛主编.—北京：清华大学出版社，2019（2024.2重印）
ISBN 978–7–302–53049–7

Ⅰ.①新…　Ⅱ.①王…　②李…　Ⅲ.①商务—英语—高等学校—教材　Ⅳ.①F7

中国版本图书馆 CIP 数据核字（2019）第 090228 号

责任编辑：徐　静
封面设计：子　一
责任校对：王凤芝
责任印制：丛怀宇

出版发行：清华大学出版社
　　　　　网　　址：https://www.tup.com.cn，https://www.wqxuetang.com
　　　　　地　　址：北京清华大学学研大厦A座　　邮　编：100084
　　　　　社 总 机：010–83470000　　邮　购：010–62786544
　　　　　投稿与读者服务：010–62776969，c-service@tup.tsinghua.edu.cn
　　　　　质 量 反 馈：010–62772015，zhiliang@tup.tsinghua.edu.cn
印 装 者：北京盛通印刷股份有限公司
经　　销：全国新华书店
开　　本：210mm×285mm　印　张：12.25　字　数：382千字
版　　次：2019年8月第1版　印　次：2024年2月第2次印刷
定　　价：59.00元

产品编号：078731–01

Preface

改革开放 40 年，商务英语专业创办 10 年来，全国已有 367 所高校开设了商务英语本科专业，商务英语人才培养在我国已初具规模，商务英语人才培养体系不断完善，一个突出的标志就是核心课程和核心教材建设。近年来，商务英语专业教材建设的特点是：引进和原创相结合，引进了一批国际知名的经典商务英语教材，如 *Market Leader*、*Intelligent Business*、*Cambridge Business English Certificate* 等，而且，还自主开发了一批商务英语教材；其次是继承和创新相结合，在继承外语技能教学优良传统的同时，将语言、文化、商务相结合，解决了打牢英语基本功、学习文化、培养商务意识和商务素养兼顾的难题；此外，教材和课程建设同步，通过编写教材，创建了"综合商务英语"等一批新课，打造出"金课"，有力地推动了商务英语专业核心课程和教材建设。

根据 2018 年教育部颁布的《普通高等学校外国语言文学类本科专业教学质量国家标准》的要求，商务英语专业必须开设 17 门核心课程，其中最重要的一门课程就是"综合商务英语"。该课程是商务英语专业基础阶段的英语技能主干课程，对打牢学生的商务英语基本功、拓展商务文化、培养商务意识和商务素养极为重要。

针对"综合商务英语"主干核心课程，清华大学出版社引进了著名的剑桥商务英语经典教材，并按国家标准的要求，组织强大的商务英语教材编写团队，经过精心改编，推出了"新时代商务英语综合教程"。这套教材具有以下六个特点：

第一，原版引进著名的剑桥商务英语教材，该教材编写和出版质量高，在国外面世后多次再版，多年畅销，经久不衰，堪称经典。

第二，改编后的教材共分为 4 册，适合 1~2 年级"综合商务英语"课程 4 个学期使用，每学期使用 1 册。每册 8 个单元，4 册共 32 个单元，每个单元包含 2 篇课文，适用于每周 4

个学时的课堂教学使用。

第三，所有单元的主题都与真实职场和商务活动密切相关，并经过精心编排，教材主题由浅入深，既相互联系，又相对独立。课文选材短小精悍，图文并茂，语篇鲜活，可读性极强，并配有充足的练习题，练习任务设计丰富而实用，兼顾词汇、语法、听说、写作、翻译、商务知识、商务文化、商务沟通等各方面。

第四，对引进教材做适当改编，以符合中国英语教学的特点和需求。此外，还增加了全英文的商务知识点和商务翻译，前者扩展学生的商务知识，后者训练学生英汉互译的能力，弥补了教材背景知识不足、没有翻译练习的缺陷。

第五，为第3册和第4册教材精心编配了商务案例分析单元，训练学生以问题为导向，以案例为对象，提高商务环境下分析问题和解决问题的能力。

第六，针对全国商务英语专业四级考试的题型和要求，教材练习部分增加了与四级考试相关的题型，帮助学生熟悉和了解四级考试的形式和难度。

本套教材适合全国商务英语专业应用型本科院校作为"综合商务英语"课程教材使用，也适合高职高专商务英语专业选用，同时也可作为经管类专业学生的专业英语教材，以及商务英语爱好者和企业员工英语培训使用。本套教材的改编得到了对外经济贸易大学、西南财经大学、华中农业大学、山东财经大学、安徽财经大学等高校的专家和清华大学出版社的领导和编辑的大力支持，在此表示衷心感谢。

谨以此纪念改革开放40年商务英语的发展，是为序。

北京语言大学教授、博士生导师

王立非

2019年1月于北京

Contents

UNIT **1** Work roles

Warming up

 How much do you know about the following jobs? Describe the major responsibilities of each.

CEO	marketing manager	accountant	consultant
HR manager	sales executive	financial advisor	

 Discuss with your partner about the possible responsibilities you may take in your career in the future.

Text A Work roles

Five employees describe their jobs.

1 ▷ I've just moved from a company with a very strict hierarchy to a fast-growing software company and it's been hard coming to terms with the changes. I mean, don't get me wrong, I enjoy my new job a lot more. I have a lot more responsibility now and everything's done in project teams and managed by objectives. The one thing I do miss, however, is that now, once a project's running, the team's pretty much on its own and left to solve any problems by itself. Before, there was always a superior I could turn to for help, and to be honest, I'd be much happier if that were still the case. Especially when you're starting a new job, having someone to talk to can make things a lot easier.

2 ▷ I produce technical documents, you know, users' manuals and that sort of thing—nothing creative, I'm afraid. Our team's responsible for its own work schedules. And as long as everything's finished before the machine's shipped, it's up to us when we do it. So you'd think with email and everything, we'd all be able to work from home or come and go as we please—but that's not the case. Unfortunately, it's a very conservative company so everyone's still clocking in and out at the same time. I suppose the managers have always worked a routine nine to five and just can't imagine anything else being possible.

3 ▷ I'm an IT consultant and I'm working for a small leisure group on a one-year contract. So I'm travelling around Europe a lot, which I know sounds very glamorous, but it's just a case of jetting in, fixing a hotel's

computer and then jetting out again. It also means I'm on call and work very… shall we say "flexible" hours, including many weekends. Oh and I'm also responsible for the website, which I work on from home. What I miss is support from colleagues, you know, being able to discuss problems or things like the latest technology with other IT professionals in the same job. So, yes, it's definitely the social side of my job I'd like to improve.

4 ▶ Well, I'm a temp and I'm working as a PA for a law firm in London just now. It's a medium-sized firm that's grown quickly so its organisation is very much like that of a smaller company. OK, I know it's unreasonable to expect a definite job description—I mean, if something needs doing, then I think whoever's available should do it. But I'm already responsible for managing the diaries and correspondence of two senior managers, so when the telephone's ringing all day and people keep asking me to photocopy reports or even make them coffee, it just becomes impossible to get anything done.

5 ▶ I work for the U.K. subsidiary of a Japanese company and it's very Japanese in terms of the way it's run. I've just got a new boss, who's come over from Japan. We seem to be getting on pretty well at the moment—he always has time for me and gives me lots of support. The only thing is, I don't really have a huge say in what I do—which is all right but sometimes it would be nice to be able to show a bit of initiative. Our work processes are totally standardised as fixed routines, which I don't mind. It's just that I always have to consult him before I can make even the smallest alteration to any job of any sort.

Words and expressions

alteration /ˌɔːltə'reɪʃən/	n.	改变，更改	be on call	随叫随到
glamorous /'glæmərəs/	adj.	令人向往的	be up to	取决于
hierarchy /'haɪəˌrɑːkɪ/	n.	等级制度	clock in and out	打卡上 / 下班
initiative /ɪ'nɪʃɪətɪv/	n.	主动权	flexible hours	弹性工作时间
jet /dʒet/	v.	急冲；乘喷气式	get on well	相处融洽
		飞机飞行	have a say	有发言权
manual /'mænjʊəl/	n.	手册，指南	IT consultant	信息技术顾问
routine /ruː'tiːn/	n.	日常工作	leisure group	旅游休闲集团公司
superior /sjuː'pɪərɪə(r)/	n.	上级	PA (Personal Assistant)	私人助理
temp /temp/	n.	临时雇员		

Comprehension tasks

Read the text and decide which improvement each employee would most like to see.

1. _____
2. _____
3. _____
4. _____
5. _____

a. more responsibility
b. more team work
c. fewer routine tasks
d. more flexible hours
e. fewer interruptions
f. clearer objectives
g. more creative work
h. more managerial support

Read the text again and answer the following questions.

1. Why does the first employee enjoy his job so much? What do you suppose is the reason he changed his job?

2. What are the job responsibilities of the second employee? Is there any way to make the job more creative?

3. What is the pace of the third employee's job? Does it sound glamourous to you?

4. Why does the fourth employee think that it is unreasonable to expect a definite job description?

5. What does the last employee mean by saying that his company is very Japanese in terms of the way it is run?

Vocabulary

Match the words with opposite meanings by use of linking lines.

1. nimble   a. dynamic
2. static   b. hampered
3. feasible   c. focused
4. flexible   d. simple
5. complex   e. rigid
6. diverse   f. impossible

Use the noun form of the following verbs to complete the email.

brief	collaborate	respond	co-ordinate	allocate
motivate	assign	assess	balance	

RE: New sales project

From: Higgins, Alan [ajh@concam.co.uk]
Sent: Friday 7 December 10.17 p.m.
To: Brownjohn, Cornelia
Subject: RE: New sales project

Connie,

Sorry you couldn't make it to the meeting yesterday. I've attached your project [1] _brief_ outlining the strategy for the new sales project. It's going to be a tough [2] _____ with ambitious targets but I'm sure you can do it.

We've already started recruiting the new team and the [3] _____ has been great. I'll hand over all the CVs for your [4] _____. I think it's very important that we get the right [5] _____ of personalities within the team—we don't want compatibility problems that will have a negative effect on [6] _____.

I think it's vital you concentrate on team [7] _____—so don't get too "hands on" and involved on a day-to-day basis. The budget [8] _____ is quite generous so you should be able to afford to recruit the right people.

And finally, don't forget that [9] _____ with other offices is one of the prime objectives—so make sure communication channels are set up properly right at the start.

Good luck!

 Choose the correct word to fill each gap.

Research has shown that in today's dynamic working environment the traditional job description is no longer doing its job. Today's jobs are not (1) _____—they are constantly changing. This leads to (2) _____, with employees uncertain of their precise work roles. This can be illustrated by the following quotation from a job description: "Meet or exceed customer (3) _____." The initial reaction may be that this (4) _____ is perfectly clear but on closer examination it poses a number of questions. For example, is it (5) _____ employees to do whatever they feel is necessary to (6) _____ this end without restrictions? Or is it saying (7) _____ our procedures and this will be the outcome? Who knows? Perhaps the manager, but the description certainly does not (8) _____ things sufficiently from the employee's point of view.

1.	a. static	b. routine	c. standard
2.	a. disparity	b. initiative	c. ambiguity
3.	a. undertakings	b. objectives	c. expectations
4.	a. schedule	b. feedback	c. statement
5.	a. authorising	b. allocating	c. prescribing
6.	a. support	b. achieve	c. carry out
7.	a. follow	b. comply	c. serve
8.	a. highlight	b. identify	c. clarify

Listening

TASK 6 You will hear five different people talking about their jobs. Match the extracts with the departments.

1. _____
2. _____
3. _____
4. _____
5. _____

a. legal
b. sales
c. accounts
d. purchasing
e. customer service
f. despatch
g. production
h. personnel

TASK 7 Listen again and match the extracts with the complaints. For each extract, choose the speaker's main complaint about a colleague.

1. _____
2. _____
3. _____
4. _____
5. _____

a. constant interruptions.
b. personal telephone calls
c. untidiness in the office.
d. bad time-keeping
e. frequent breaks
f. food in the office
g. gossiping about staff
h. misuse of office equipment

Business communication

 Work in pairs. Discuss the following questions with your partner.

- What should a company value about its employees?
- How should a company build a team spirit in its workforce?

Translation

 Translate the following sentences into Chinese.

1. I've just moved from a company with a very strict hierarchy to a fast-growing software company and it's been hard coming to terms with the changes.

   _____

   _____

2. So I'm travelling around Europe a lot, which I know sounds very glamorous, but it's just a case of jetting in, fixing a hotel's computer and then jetting out again.

   _____

   _____

3. But I'm already responsible for managing the diaries and correspondence of two senior managers, so when the telephone's ringing all day and people keep asking me to photocopy reports or even make them coffee, it just becomes impossible to get anything done.

   _____

   _____

4. By taking the initiative, this employee doesn't wait for direction from his boss. He observes a need and he makes himself available. In addition, employees might show initiative on the job by simply speaking up and offering suggestions.

   _____

   _____

5. Organisations benefit when employees have clear goals that help meet overall business objectives. Employees who can see a clear future with a company and feel supported in their professional endeavours are more likely to want to stay with the company.

   _____

   _____

Translate the following sentences into English.

1. 考勤有助于企业主了解员工是否按实际工作时间领取报酬。考勤的关键在于记录员工的工作时间，那么员工准确、高效打卡上下班就很重要。(clock in and out)

   _____

2. 在谈到她的职业生涯计划时，这个大四的学生说她想找一个上班时间弹性大的工作，这样就可以在她精力最不济的午饭后小睡一会儿，又能在她大脑最灵敏的晚上熬夜工作。(flexible hours)

   _____

3. 刘女士是一家世界知名品牌会议与活动策划公司的主管，她说："我的朋友认为我过着光鲜的生活，到欧洲各大度假村旅行，但人们看不见你从早上 6 点忙到凌晨 2 点的那些日子。有时候，如果每天都能换换衣服你就很走运了。"(glamorous)

   _____

4. 通过建立这个子公司，我们能够更好地支持当地经济：新的子公司更适合在当地与中小企业合作，因为按它们的规模通常无法与我们合作。(subsidiary)

   _____

5. 像在大多数机构中一样，最重要的面对面的关系是上下级关系。在日本公司的组织中，这些人都是分配到同一个工作单位不同级别的员工而已。(superior)

   _____

   _____

Writing

 Make a survey on how the employees in a company actually spend their time at work. Write a report describing your findings and recommending any necessary changes.

Business know-how

Read the following passage and make an oral summary of the main points to your partner or group.

Entrepreneurship（企业家精神）

Entrepreneurship is the process of designing, launching and running a new business, which is often initially a small business. The people who create these businesses are called entrepreneurs.

Entrepreneurship has been described as the "capacity and willingness to develop, organise and manage a business venture along with any of its risks in order to make a profit". While definitions of entrepreneurship typically focus on the launching and running of businesses, due to the high risks involved in launching a start-up, a significant proportion of start-up businesses have to close due to "lack of funding, bad business decisions, an economic crisis, lack of market demand—or a combination of all of these".

A broader definition of the term is sometimes used, especially in the field of economics. In this usage, an entrepreneur is an entity which has the ability to find and act upon opportunities to translate inventions or technology into new products: "The entrepreneur is able to recognise the commercial potential of the invention and organise the capital, talent, and other resources that turn an invention into a commercially viable innovation." In this sense, the term "entrepreneurship" also captures innovative activities on the part of established firms, in addition to similar activities on the part of new businesses.

Text B Attending interviews

Barrie Watson of Belbin Associates has just led a Team Leadership Workshop at Ekstrom Engineering. The following is his report on the workshop.

Report on effective Team Leadership Workshop

The aim of this report is to summarise issues arising from the recent Team Leadership Workshop at Ekstrom and recommend appropriate action.

Findings

The workshop began with an assessment of how the Ekstrom team leaders understood their roles. Perceptions ranged from assigning and checking other people's work to motivating others to do the work. This disparity clearly showed that the team leaders had different understandings of their roles and that Ekstrom therefore needed to communicate its expectations more explicitly.

In order to do this, Ekstrom identified key tasks and used WorkSet colours to illustrate the precise level of responsibility which could be allocated to each. A task such as communicating with the team, for example, might be approached in a variety of ways:

- I give my staff instructions every morning. (Blue work)
- I let my staff decide on the best approach for themselves. (Yellow work)
- My team and I discuss how to do each job. (Orange work)

Having identified the different possible approaches to each key task, the company was able to select which was most appropriate and communicate its expectations in terms of the skills and behaviour required.

Conclusions

It is clear that Ekstrom needs to ensure that its team leaders are capable of performing key tasks in a manner compatible with company expectations. However, whilst the appropriate skills can be developed through in-company training, changing behavioural attributes is much more difficult.

Recommendations

We strongly recommend, therefore, that Ekstrom sets up assessment centres where existing team leaders and new applicants can be screened to ensure that they have the appropriate attributes for effective team leadership.

Barrie Watson
Belbin Associates

3-4 Bennell Court, Comberton, Cambridge CB3 7DS,
Telephone: 01223 264975, Facsimile: 01223 264976, email: belbin@belbin.com

Words and expressions

allocate /'æləkeɪt/	v.	分配；分派
assign /ə'saɪn/	v.	指派
attribute /'ætrɪbjuːt/	n.	特质
behavioural /bɪ'heɪvjərəl/	adj.	行为的
disparity /dɪ'spærətɪ/	n.	差异
expectation /ˌekspek'teɪʃən/	n.	期望
explicitly /ɪk'splɪsɪtlɪ/	adv.	明确地
illustrate /'ɪləstreɪt/	v.	说明，阐明

in-company /ɪn'kʌmpənɪ/	adj.	公司内部的
perception /pə'sepʃən/	n.	感知能力；洞察力
screen /skriːn/	v.	筛选
summarise /'sʌməraɪz/	v.	总结，概括
whilst /waɪlst/	conj.	当……的时候
a variety of		种种；各种各样的
be capable of		能够……，可以……

Comprehension tasks

Read the text and answer the following questions.

1. What were the team leaders asked to do first?
2. What did this show?
3. What did the use of WorkSet colours then allow the company to do?
4. Why does Barrie Watson distinguish between skills and attributes?
5. How can Ekstrom ensure its team leaders have the right attributes?

Complete the following information with phrases from the report.

Don't forget

Report writing

The following phrases are useful when writing reports.

- **Introduction**
  This report aims/sets out to...
  _____

- **Findings**
  It was found that...
  _____

- **Conclusions**
  It was decided/agreed/felt that...

  _____

- **Recommendations**
  It is suggested that...

  _____

Vocabulary

 Use the words to write sentences with *job*.

He re-aligned certain aspects of the job.

carry out

aspects   brief

highlight

communicate   responsibilities

description   (job)   classify

feedback   monitor

re-align

set up   enjoy

duties

 Which word in each group is the odd one out?

1. collaborative   remote   team-based   co-operative
2. stable   static   sequential   routine
3. responsive   dynamic   flexible   virtual
4. separate   divide   specify   break down
5. back up   resist   hamper   prevent
6. evaluation   feedback   interaction   assessment
7. accomplish   challenge   manage   achieve
8. strategy   concept   impact   plan
9. paperwork   hard copy   email   stationery
10. motivation   authority   control   supervision

Match the words and then use them to complete the sentences.

real-time	units
online	information
flexible	advantage
business	support
competitive	working
communication	structure
company	processes
operating	channels

1. Technology now gives us *real-time information* on sales as they happen so we can order products the moment we look as if we might run out of stock.
2. The company is divided into six separate _____.
3. We're assessing the effectiveness of our _____ to see whether we can improve the flow of information between project team members.
4. They've streamlined their _____ by removing some of the layers of hierarchy in senior management.
5. I don't think the new _____ policies have increased productivity, but letting employees work from home has certainly improved morale.
6. Our web team will provide the _____ for the new product.
7. We're hoping that by producing in the Czech Republic we can get good quality at good prices, which will give us a _____ over our rivals.
8. She wants us to review our _____ to find out how we can reduce production times and waste levels.

Speaking

Work in pairs. Discuss with your partner what's your ideal job. Then discuss the following information about your ideal job.

- position
- responsibilities
- duties

Form a pair and discuss the following topic with your partner.

Do you think it is important to define professional boundaries of work roles? Why?

Business communication

 Use the framework below to plan a one-minute talk on the following topic. Then work in pairs and make a presentation.

Communication: How to ensure good communication within teams

Opening sentence: _____

_____

Main points   Supporting ideas

- _____   - _____

- _____   - _____

- _____   - _____

Concluding sentence: _____

Translation

 Translate the following sentences into Chinese.

1. The aim of this report is to summarise issues arising from the recent Team Leadership Workshop at Ekstrom and recommend appropriate action.

   _____

   _____

2. This disparity clearly showed that the team leaders had different understandings of their roles and that Ekstrom therefore needed to communicate its expectations more explicitly.

   _____

   _____

3. Having identified the different possible approaches to each key task, the company was able to select which was most appropriate and communicate its expectations in terms of the skills and behavior required.

_____

_____

4. By the time an offer has been procured, most job candidates have researched their potential employer from angles such as organisational viability, management's expectations, opportunities for growth, etc., but they may fail to examine their compatibility with an organisation's corporate culture.

_____

_____

5. There are no legal reasons to prevent an employee from claiming sick pay for a job which they are currently medically unfit to carry out, whilst working for another completely separate job, which they are medically fit for.

_____

_____

TASK 10 Translate the following sentences into English.

1. 大多数雇主没有明确地在招聘广告中公布工资，而有些公司会在招聘广告中公布工资，那些公布工资的职位有其显著的特征。(explicitly)

_____

_____

2. 他建议雇佣一个学生团队来做一个公司的项目，让他们分析公司的问题，提出一个完整的报告，并给出切实可行的建议。(in-company)

_____

_____

3. 兼职意味着一个人每周固定工作时间从几个小时到30个小时不等。例如，一个学生可以在每个星期六工作8个小时来勤工俭学。(rang from)

_____

_____

4. 当你想要填补职位空缺时，你很可能会有几个应聘者。下一步你将筛选求职者，这意味着你应该首先明确谁是申请人，然后复函确认。(screen)

_____

_____

5. 在一些国家，如果同一个岗位的工资有差异，雇主必须提供除性别以外的正当理由，否则雇主可能会陷入深深的麻烦之中。（disparity）

_____

_____

Writing

 Suppose you have been asked to write a report on how communication could be improved within your project team. You have made the following notes to help you plan your report. Use the notes to write a report.

Notes on planning a report

Report making recommendations

- Start with an introduction

  aim—to identify problems with communication within the team & make recommendations on how to improve it

- Findings—state your main points & give one or more supporting ideas for each main point

  1) whole team rarely gets together

  2) people in different departments are in different parts of the building

  3) people don't copy emails to other team members

- Conclusion—summarise your main points

  1) improving procedures will improve attitudes among team members

  2) no real reason why communication shouldn't be better

- Recommendation—say what action needs to be taken

  1) schedule weekly meetings

  2) ensure people are copied in on emails

  3) organise a team-building seminar

  Don't forget to lay it out in separate paragraphs with headings!!

UNIT 2 Headhunting

Warming up

 How do you understand the cartoon below? Share your comment with your partner.

 What are the advantages and disadvantages of the following?

- internal recruitment
- job advertisements
- recruitment agencies
- headhunting

Text A) Why do people headhunt?

"The reason headhunting works is because we target the individual," says Adelaide Macaulay of London-based Morgan Howard International. "If a company needs to fill a niche role in a niche market, then they'll come to us." Macaulay recruits for a number of clients spread throughout Europe. Each company needs to fill an important or highly-specialised role and thinks traditional advertising would not be effective. This is particularly the case as 99 percent of the people Macaulay targets are not actively on the market. She usually targets people who are happy in their job and not looking to move. However, an Achilles heel can usually be found that allows the headhunter to persuade them that they are, in fact, wanting to change. It may be that they are fed up with the company, that they want more money, or that they want a change of location.

Internet headhunting firm Netsearch is more blunt than Macaulay about the reason why companies turn to headhunters: "Headhunting is relatively cheap and on the increase as selection gets worse and worse." Recruiters divide their business into "selection" and "search" processes. The former category refers to traditional advertising and the latter to the activities of the headhunter. Recruitment officers believe that for certain vacancies advertising is too expensive and throws up hundreds of largely unsuitable CVs, which take hours to process. Headhunters, on the other hand, have enough tricks up their sleeve to produce a shorter, better quality list of candidates. With Netsearch, they insist, you can get a better person more quickly.

Headhunters are understandably unwilling to reveal their methods. However, one source did claim that if he had one name and extension number, within a matter of hours he would have a good idea of who everyone in the department is and what they do. If, for example, the original contract is unavailable, a colleague will answer the phone and happily divulge their own name. By a simple process of deduction, it is then easy to work out that person's position in the company; if people are sitting at adjacent desks, the chances are that they are in similar roles. With clever questioning, the headhunter can navigate around the rest of the department and quickly compile a list of names and likely job roles. This information can then be stored for future reference.

One thing all of this makes clear is the importance of names. They are the currency by which headhunting operates. Any name a headhunter comes across is written down and put on record. This process has been made much easier with the invention of email, which indicates a person's name, employer and even the department they work in. Anyone contributing to an online newsgroup with informed, specialist opinion may well become the target of a headhunter. Companies like Netsearch constantly monitor such forums hunting for potential candidates.

Words and expressions

adjacent /ə'dʒeɪsənt/	adj.	邻近的	
blunt /blʌnt/	adj.	直率的	
compile /kəm'paɪl/	v.	编制；编写	
deduction /dɪ'dʌkʃən/	n.	推理	
divulge /daɪ'vʌldʒ/	v.	泄露	
extension /ɪk'stenʃən/	n.	电话分机	
headhunt /'hedhʌnt/	v.	物色（人才）	
informed /ɪn'fɔːmd/	adj.	有学问的；有见地的	
navigate /'nævɪgeɪt/	adj.	行走；浏览	

reveal /rɪ'viːl/	v.	揭示
target /'tɑːrgɪt/	v.	把……作为目标
Achilles heel		阿喀琉斯之踵（致命的弱点）
be fed up with		对……感到厌烦
come across		偶然发现；偶然遇见
niche market		利基市场（小的有利可图的市场）
throw up		放弃
tricks up one's sleeve		锦囊妙计

Comprehension tasks

 Read the first two paragraphs of the text. Match the sentences with the functions.

1. This is particularly the case as 99 per cent of the people Macaulay targets are not actively on the market.

2. It may be that they are fed up with the company, that they want more money, or that they want a change of location.

3. Internet headhunting firm Netsearch is more blunt than Macaulay about the reason why companies turn to headhunters.

4. The former category refers to traditional advertising and the latter to the activities of the headhunter.

5. Headhunters, on the other hand, have enough tricks up their sleeve to produce a shorter, better quality list of candidates.

   a. explaining
   b. comparing
   c. emphasising
   d. contrasting
   e. exemplifying

Read the text again and circle "True" or "False". Correct the false statements.

1. Macaulay works for some European companies which find that job advertising does not fill a niche role.   True/False

2. Macaulay often targets the people who feel bored at what they have been doing at the present position.   True/False

3. With headhunting, you can get a better person more quickly because it helps screen unsuitable CVs more effectively.   True/False

4. A professional headhunter is usually skilled in asking smart questions and good at logical thinking.   True/False

5. Headhunters often attend forums held in different places in order to search for candidates who are able to contribute informed opinions.   True/False

Vocabulary

Complete each sentence with a suitable preposition.

1. Headhunting is _____ the increase as advertising becomes less and less cost-effective.

2. Headhunters are able to target people who are not actually _____ the job market.

3. A headhunter will always make a careful note of names _____ future reference.

4. Recruitment in the U.K. is divided _____ agency recruitment, advertising or executive search.

5. Headhunters can offer companies access _____ commercially sensitive information.

6. Executive search firms monitor Internet forums, noting any interesting names they come _____ .

7. The headhunter assists _____ the offer process.

8. You don't need to be fed up _____ your job to be susceptible to an approach from a headhunter.

9. A brilliant contribution _____ an Internet forum could possibly attract the attention of a headhunter.

Match the words.

1. fill   a list
2. present   a vacancy
3. shortlist   business
4. pay   findings
5. conduct   a retainer
6. compile   candidates

 Use the words to write sentences with *recruit/recruitment*.

Candidates go through our recruitment process.

apply   agency

qualities   candidates   process

sector   method

job   **recruit/recruitment**   skills

CV   performance   shortlist

appoint   vacancy

headhunter

Listening

Terrain Ltd., a leisurewear manufacturer, is investigating staff motivation. Listen to five employees talking to the HR Manager. Which grievance does each speaker refer to?

1. _____ 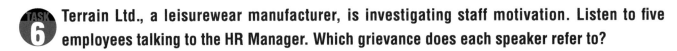   4. _____

2. _____   5. _____

3. _____

     a. too much responsibility
     b. uninteresting work
     c. lack of communication
     d. uncooperative colleagues
     e. lack of recognition
     f. unsatisfactory pay
     g. inflexible working hours
     h. lack of clear objectives

TASK 7 Listen again and complete the Findings section of the report by summarising the grievances of the Terrain employees.

Report on staff motivation

Introduction
This report presents the results of the recent survey of staff motivation. The findings are based on interviews with employees from all departments within the company.

Findings

Conclusion
It is clear that there are significant levels of dissatisfaction regarding certain issues within the company. Unless these issues are addressed as a matter of urgency, the consequent demotivation of staff will undoubtedly have a negative impact on the performance of the company.

Recommendations

→Ellough Industrial Estate ➤ BECCLES → Suffolk ✿ NR34 7RY ✒ Tel 01502 714281 ◆ Fax 01502 714282 ✿

Business communication

 Work in groups. Hold a meeting within your team to discuss about how to identify an excellent candidate.

Useful language for meeting

Introducing the topic of the meeting
The main reason for this meeting is...

What we need to decide/talk about/think about today is...

The (main) topic/subject/aim/objective/purpose/goal of this meeting is...

Asking for opinions
What do you think (about this/about that)?

Does anyone have any (other/particular) thoughts/comments/opinions/views (on this)?

Giving opinions
I really think...

I strongly believe/I really believe/I firmly believe...

I'm no expert on this, but...

(I'm not sure/certain, but) I would guess/I would imagine/I would suppose...

This is only my opinion, but...

I would probably say that...

Agreeing
I totally agree.

Exactly/Absolutely!

I feel just the same way.

I suppose you're right./I guess you're right.

Disagreeing
(I'm sorry but) I really don't agree.

(I'm afraid) I have to disagree.

I mostly agree, but...

(That's a) good point, but...

Making suggestions
I would suggest/I would recommend/I would advise...

My (main) suggestion/recommendation/advice would be to...

The best solution/The best course of action would probably be...

We should (probably) consider/think about...

Translate the following sentences into Chinese.

1. She usually targets people who are happy in their job and not looking to move. However, an Achilles heel can usually be found that allows the headhunter to persuade them that they are, in fact, wanting to change.

   _____

   _____

2. Recruitment officers believe that for certain vacancies advertising is too expensive and throws up hundreds of largely unsuitable CVs, which take hours to process. Headhunters, on the other hand, have enough tricks up their sleeve to produce a shorter, better quality list of candidates.

   _____

   _____

3. However, one source did claim that if he had one name and extension number, within a matter of hours he would have a good idea of who everyone in the department is and what they do.

   _____

   _____

4. Being visible to headhunters is a great way of ensuring you don't miss out on the best career opportunities. One of the tips is to get involved in activity such as attending conferences, industry forums and working groups.

   _____

   _____

5. We'll help you navigate through the world of executive search, helping you decode the best options for your situation—whether hiring top talent for your firm or looking for your next sales job, we'll take the mystery out of working with a headhunter.

   _____

   _____

Translate the following sentences into English.

1. 如果某家公司的员工被猎头看中，他们很可能就会离开那家公司，因为另一家公司已经接近了他们，并给他们提供了另一份薪酬、地位都更高的工作。(headhunt)

   _____

   _____

2. 重要的是要制造出神秘感,让候选者亲自回到招聘人员那里。如果过快发送电子邮件或推特帖子泄露过多的信息,可能会错失良机。(divulge)

_____

_____

3. 许多人致电招聘者,请他们帮忙寻找生命科学领域的工作。然而,他们并没有意识到,招聘者往往只专注于某一领域,因此无法帮助所有打电话的人。(niche)

_____

_____

4. 付费广告使招聘者能够针对特定受众,由此也提供了一个将招聘内容直接投放到最有效的地方的机会。(target)

_____

_____

5. 我们的业务范围包括职能、业务单元和部门分析,并允许企业在做出招聘决定之前,以洞悉的国际化眼光看待市场中存在的事物。(informed)

_____

_____

Writing

 Complete the report in Task 7 on Page 27 by making your recommendations to address the grievances.

Business know-how

Read the following passage and illustrate the importance of human resource management orally to your partner.

Human resource management（人力资源管理）

Human resource management (HRM or **HR)** is the strategic approach to the effective management of organisation workers so that they help the business gain a competitive advantage. the HR Department is designed to maximise employee performance in service of an employer's strategic objectives. HR is primarily concerned with the management of people within organisations, focusing on policies and on systems. The HR Department is responsible for overseeing employee-benefits design, employee recruitment, training and development, performance appraisal, and rewarding (e.g., managing pay and benefit systems). HR also concerns itself with organisational change and industrial relations, that is, the balancing of organisational practices with requirements arising from collective bargaining and from governmental laws.

HR's overall purpose is to ensure that the organisation is able to achieve success through people. HR professionals manage the human capital of an organisation and focus on implementing policies and processes. They can specialise in recruiting, training, employee-relations or benefits. Recruiting specialists find and hire top talents. Training and development professionals ensure that employees are trained and have continuous development. This is done through training programs, performance evaluations and reward programs. Employee relations deals with concerns of employees when policies are violated, such as in cases involving harassment or discrimination. Someone in benefits develops compensation structures, family-leave programs, discounts and other benefits that employees can get. On the other side of the field are Human Resources Generalists or business partners. These human-resources professionals could work in all areas or be labour-relations representatives working with unionised employees.

Text B Headhunting

Dave Archer specialises in executive search in the IT sector from the executive search firm ArcherGoodall Associates. The following is his presentation about headhunting.

Good afternoon. My name's Dave Archer and I'm here to tell you a little bit today about how the executive search process works. Now in Europe the executive search industry is worth $10bn a year, with a lot of that business being conducted in the U.K. U.K. recruiters basically use one of four methods: there's agency recruitment, advertising selection (which is advertising in newspapers), a combination of selection and search and, at the top-end, executive search, otherwise known as headhunting. The executive search market is particularly prevalent in areas where market growth has been driven by skills shortages in client companies who are in a constant process of change. This is particularly the case in the finance, consulting and IT sectors, for example.

There's a fairly standard operating procedure for the delivery of headhunting assignments. It begins with a client giving a headhunter exclusive instruction and a brief to fill a vacancy. The headhunter's first task is to target potential companies, then individuals within those companies, either through desk research or through extensive contact networks. The headhunter then speaks to those individuals who match the specified criteria closely and are most appropriate for the job in question.

The headhunter then meets a number of potential candidates, either at their own offices or at a neutral location. Of course, these meetings have to be arranged and held with the utmost discretion. The headhunter then puts together the curriculum vitaes and presents his findings to the client. At this meeting the client is given a shortlist of about eight candidates and selects three or four of them for interview. This number gives a good chance of a successful candidate being hired. The candidates then go through the client's own interview procedure, possibly along with other candidates that applied directly to the company in response to an advertisement. Afterwards, the headhunter gives professional advice to both sides and facilitates the offer process to make sure that the whole assignment ends with a successful hire.

As for remuneration, the headhunter will receive a proportion, usually about 30 percent, of the first annual salary of the person appointed. When a search company has been given an exclusive instruction to fill a vacancy, payment is normally billed in three instalments: first of all a retainer, then a second instalment upon submission of the shortlist and finally, a completion fee when the appointee starts with the client.

Now the advantage of a good headhunter is that he can provide a clear understanding of the business environment, a client's activities, their strengths and weaknesses and those of their rivals. This kind of comprehensive information can only be obtained through painstaking detective work, a close relationship with the key players in the industry and an international presence.

Headhunting is considered by many to be a "black art" at best, unethical at worst. Yet at its highest levels, search is time and cost-efficient and provides a client with commercially sensitive information which would be otherwise unavailable. It targets those people who are happy in their current position, motivated and able to consistently deliver top performance—in other words, just the people who can benefit the client's growth plans and who cannot be accessed in any other way.

Words and expressions

brief /briːf/	*n.*	摘要，简报	**proportion** /prəˈpɔːʃən/	*n.*	部分；比例
cost-efficient /ˈkɒstɪˈfiʃənt/	*adj.*	有成本效益的；合算的	**remuneration** /rɪˌmjuːnəˈreɪʃən/	*n.*	酬劳；酬金
			retainer /rɪˈteɪmə(r)/	*n.*	预付费用
detective /dɪˈtektɪv/	*adj.*	侦查的；探测的	**top-end** /ˌtɒpˈend/	*adj.*	高端的
discretion /dɪˈskreʃən/	*n.*	谨慎	**unethical** /ʌnˈeθɪkl/	*adj.*	缺德的
exclusive /ɪkˈskluːsɪv/	*adj.*	独有的；单独的	**utmost** /ˈʌtməʊst/	*adj.*	极度的
facilitate /fəˈsɪlɪteɪt/	*v.*	促进；帮助；使容易	**annual salary**		年薪
			black art		妖术，魔法
instalment /ɪnˈstɔːlmənt/	*n.*	分期付款	**completion fee**		完成费
neutral /ˈnjuːtrəl/	*adj.*	中立的	**contact network**		人脉关系
painstaking /ˈpeɪnzteɪkɪŋ/	*adj.*	艰苦的；勤勉的	**desk research**		案头工作
prevalent /ˈprevələnt/	*adj.*	普遍的			

Comprehension tasks

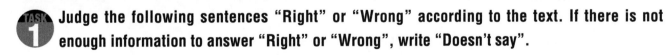

Judge the following sentences "Right" or "Wrong" according to the text. If there is not enough information to answer "Right" or "Wrong", write "Doesn't say".

1. Headhunting is also called executive search. _____

2. Headhunting is popular in sectors like finance because such an industry is changing rapidly.
   _____

3. In a standard headhunting process, the headhunter initially targets potential candidates and then makes a shortlist for the client. _____

4. The candidates are always interviewed separately in some carefully chosen places. _____

5. The first annual salary of the hired person is often 30 percent higher than his previous pay. _____

6. A good headhunter is capable of analysing his client's business conditions and gathering important information through personal channels. _____

7. Headhunting is viewed as a "black art" since it aims to steal the best talent from a business organisation that provides a good working environment for that talent. _____

2 **Put the following stages of the headhunting process in the correct order.**

☐ **a.** The headhunter assists with the final contract negotiations.

☐ **b.** The headhunter researches potential companies to identify candidates.

☐ **c.** The client pays the headhunter the final balance of his/her fee.

☐ **d.** The headhunter interviews potential candidates and draws up a shortlist.

☐ **e.** The client instructs the headhunter to fill a vacancy and pays a retainer.

☐ **f.** The headhunter presents findings to the client.

☐ **g.** The client interviews the most promising candidates from the shortlist.

☐ **h.** The headhunter targets individuals within these companies.

☐ **i.** The client pays the second instalment of the headhunter's fee.

☐ **j.** The chosen candidate signs a contract of employment.

Vocabulary

3 **Which word in each group does not go with the word in capital letters?**

1. JOB

   rotation   satisfaction   behaviour   enrichment

2. STAFF

   motivation   criteria   car park   feedback

3. TEAM

   appointee   spirit   building   leader

4. EXECUTIVE

   search   forces   position   salary

5. ONLINE

    newsgroup   advertising   recruitment   candidate

 Put each adjective in the correct group according to the prefix that forms its opposite.

| competent | ethical | formal | satisfactory | discreet |
| appropriate | co-operative | flexible | enthusiastic | |

in-	un-
incompetent	

 Use the positive or negative forms of the words in the box in Task 4 to complete the sentences below.

1. He's _____! He just doesn't know how to do the job properly!
2. She's a very _____ member of the team—always willing to help people.
3. Wasim was pretty _____ about his promotion. He didn't look happy at all.
4. This is just an _____ spoken warning. Next time it will go on your record.
5. Your promotion might upset some people so be _____ about it for a while.
6. If the terms of the contract are _____, please sign and return it to us.
7. Li can be a bit _____ at times and needs to try doing things differently.
8. We'll never recruit a top manager, offering such an _____ salary.
9. Exploiting company expenses is at least _____ and possibly a sacking offence.

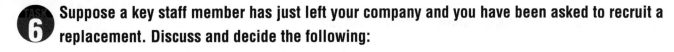

Speaking

 Suppose a key staff member has just left your company and you have been asked to recruit a replacement. Discuss and decide the following:

- the qualities required for the job;
- the best method of recruiting a replacement.

Form a pair and discuss the following questions with your partner.

Would you like to be a potential candidate of a headhunter? Why or why not?

Business communication

 Plan a one-minute talk on the importance of providing staff training, using the following checklist to help you.

 Don't forget

Planning short talks

Remember these points when planning a short talk.

- **Purpose**
  What is the purpose of the talk? (e.g. to explain a procedure)
- **Content**
  What are the main points?
  How are these points supported?
- **Organisation**
  How could you order your main points?
  (e.g. chronological sequence)
  How could you introduce and conclude your talk?
- **Language**
  What linking words and phrases could you use?
  What other useful phrases could you use?

Translation

 Translate the following sentences into Chinese.

1. The executive search market is particularly prevalent in areas where market growth has been driven by skills shortages in client companies who are in a constant process of change.

_____

_____

2. This kind of comprehensive information can only be obtained through painstaking detective work, a close relationship with the key players in the industry and an international presence.

    _____

    _____

3. It targets those people who are happy in their current position, motivated and able to consistently deliver top performance—in other words, just the people who can benefit the client's growth plans and who cannot be accessed in any other way.

    _____

    _____

4. We understand the need for discretion during the recruiting process, and we work closely with all parties to maintain confidentiality, ensuring that information is accessible only to those authorised to protect candidate information as well as our referral sources and client partners.

    _____

    _____

5. Sites such as LinkedIn is a boon for our researchers as they can mine the data according to industry, qualifications, seniority, company names, etc., and create useful lists of potential targets extremely quickly depending upon the client brief.

    _____

    _____

TASK 10 Translate the following sentences into English.

1. 金融企业还需从各方面先行考察猎头平台的成本效率，确定无误后再确立双方合作关系，这样才能让付出的酬劳获得同样的价值回报。(cost-efficient)

    _____

    _____

2. 猎头公司从来不帮那些找不到工作的人找工作，而是帮那些从来不愁找工作的人找工作，和银行选择贷款对象的标准一样。(criteria)

    _____

    _____

3. 国外的猎头公司往往是签署独家猎头服务协议；在中国，企业往往会与多家猎头公司签约同时进行高端人才寻访服务。(exclusive)

    _____

    _____

4. 招聘会的最大好处是招聘者和应聘者之间可以面对面地直接进行互动式交流，这有利于双方达成协议。(facilitate)

    _____

    _____

5. 每一个猎头都需要帮助自己的客户找到优质的人才，但在我们的传统文化与意识中，"挖墙脚"是不地道的。（unethical）

_____

_____

Writing

 Find a job advertisement and write a letter of application. Include your reasons for applying and explain what you can bring to the job.

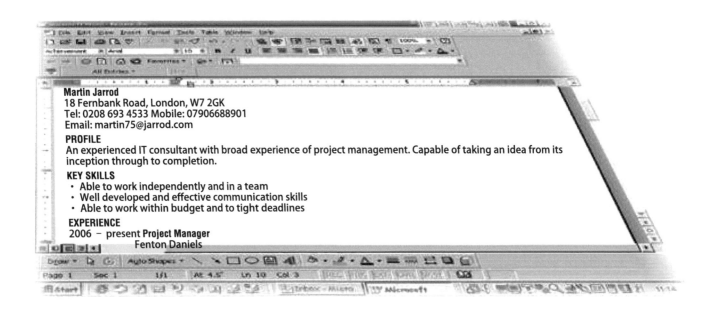

Martin Jarrod
18 Fernbank Road, London, W7 2GK
Tel: 0208 693 4533 Mobile: 07906688901
Email: martin75@jarrod.com
PROFILE
An experienced IT consultant with broad experience of project management. Capable of taking an idea from its inception through to completion.
KEY SKILLS
 · Able to work independently and in a team
 · Well developed and effective communication skills
 · Able to work within budget and to tight deadlines
EXPERIENCE
2006 – present **Project Manager**
            Fenton Daniels

UNIT 3 Entering a market

Warming up

 What research would a company do before entering a foreign market in your opinion?

 Discuss with your partner the possible approaches to entering a foreign market.

Text A Doing business in China

Britain in China, 184 Portland Place, London, W1B 1NE | www.britainchina.gov.uk

With one of the world's fastest rates of economic growth and a population of about 1.34 billion, China is an ideal market to do business with. U.K. exports to China hit a record high in September last year, reaching £743 million. Although imports from China in the same month reached £2.6 billion, the increase in exports came as good news to U.K. companies who had seen a reduction in their sales to the Asian giant in the preceding year. The Olympics in 2008 provided a valuable bridge between Beijing and London, with U.K. firms playing a key role in the design and engineering work on the Olympic stadia, as well as the new airport terminal. Now in 2011 the U.K. is continuing to encourage both export and import businesses with China.

The U.K.'s strengths match China's needs, particularly in electrical and mechanical equipment, financial services, environmental and aviation technology and vehicles. Between July and September 2010 the overseas sales of trucks and aircraft parts pushed exports to China past the £2 billion mark for the first time ever. Opportunities exist for an ever increasing number of U.K. companies, yet many fail as they do not put sufficient time and effort into understanding some fundamental differences between the two cultures. Success in China is possible, but will require long-term commitment and the ability to research the market.

Thousands of British companies have achieved a great deal in China, initially in the south, but now throughout the country. However there are a number of strategies for working with the Chinese market and it is vital to recognise the importance of the differences between the Western and Eastern ways of doing business. Ignorance of these cultural differences underlies many misunderstandings arising from business negotiations. Building relationships with prospective business partners is vital for the most successful commercial transactions. Virtually all transactions in China result from the careful cultivation of the Chinese partner by the foreign one, until a relationship of trust evolves. Earning respect is essential and once a successful relationship has been established, commercial transactions will follow. Take time to get to know your prospective business partner, go to trade fairs, visit factories and find a reliable Chinese ally to work with you. An effective Chinese colleague will often be able to work out who in the other negotiating team holds real power, not always the boss, and help smooth out any possible problems. It will almost always be necessary to visit the market and the presence of a Westerner should also be exploited to the full. Chinese businessmen will often see a visit by a foreigner as an indication of sincerity and commitment by the Western company.

Words and expressions

ally /'ælaɪ/	n.	同盟者；支持者	
aviation /ˌeɪvɪ'eɪʃən/	n.	航空	
cultivation /ˌkʌltɪ'veɪʃən/	n.	培养	
evolve /ɪ'vɒlv/	v.	发展	
exploit /ɪk'splɔɪt/	v.	利用	
hit /hɪt/	v.	达到（某水平）	
indication /ˌɪndɪ'keɪʃən/	n.	迹象，表现	
preceding /prɪ'siːdɪŋ/	adj.	在前的	
prospective /prə'spektɪv/	adj.	预期的，未来的	
stadium /'steɪdɪəm/（复数 stadia）	n.	体育场	

sufficient /sə'fɪʃənt/	adj.	足够的	
transaction /træn'zækʃən/	n.	交易	
underlie /ˌʌndə'laɪ/	v.	作为……的原因	
vital /'vaɪtl/	adj.	至关重要的	
airport terminal		机场航站楼，航空总站	
record high		历史新高	
smooth out		消除	
to the full		充分地	

Comprehension tasks

Read the text again and finish the following statements.

1. The article might come from _____.
2. The text is aimed at _____.

Read the text again and answer the following questions.

1. Why is the U.K. so important to China?
2. Which industries in China offer most potential for U.K. companies?
3. What can cause problems for companies attempting to do trade with China?
4. Which qualities are necessary for success in China?
5. Why is it advisable for exporters to visit China?

Vocabulary

3 Find words in the unit which go after business.

business   _partners_

          _____

          _____

          _____

          _____

          _____

          _____

4 Complete the sentences with the following phrases.

amount to	respond to	enquire about	allow for
invest in	intend to	participate in	build on

1. Many U.K. financial service companies are particularly keen to _____ China.
2. Ensure that you warn your hosts in advance if you _____ use audio-visual equipment.
3. This year direct U.K. exports to China are estimated to _____ well over £1bn.
4. Having entered China, many U.K. companies are now looking to _____ their success.
5. When entering the Chinese market, a company has to _____ regional differences.
6. Another tip for companies is to _____ as many local trade fairs and exhibitions as possible.
7. Mailshots are not advisable as the Chinese rarely _____ them.
8. Visitors should _____ the host's children as the family counts above all else in China.

5 Complete the following text by adding the necessary articles.

At meetings with Chinese, leader of your group will be expected to enter first and will generally be offered seat beside most senior Chinese person present. This person will usually chair meeting and act as host. At beginning of meeting, all people present will greet each other and swap business cards, after which period of small talk begins. Host will then officially start proceedings with brief introduction to Chinese enterprise. Visiting team is then invited to speak. It is appropriate at this point for foreign participants to make their case and answer questions. Following meeting Chinese enterprise will probably arrange special dinner for overseas guests along with other entertainment such as sightseeing. Guests should always accept these invitations as small talk in social setting is essential for forging relationships with Chinese.

Listening

TASK 6 Jason Labone from Hinton and Bailey, an economic research consultancy, is speaking at a conference called to discuss current economic trends. Listen and complete the notes with up to three words.

Hinton & Bailey

Introduction

1. These observations have been made during the course of my work providing _____ data for businesses in the U.K.

2. The talk will discuss the reasons for the recent _____ of mergers and acquisitions and look at how they differ from those which took place before the financial crisis of 2008.

Reasons for increase in M and A

3. There has been a noticeable _____ in the majority of industries since the onset of recession.

4. With markets in a downturn, it has become more difficult for businesses to find opportunities for _____.

5. In the financial sector, larger businesses have become _____, while smaller players have struggled with increased costs.

6. Smaller financial institutions have found it necessary to merge as the industry goes through a _____.

Changes in M and A since 2008

7. Since 2008, banks are feeling pressure to move the economy out of recession, now that they have been _____ by government.

8. Now more cautious with risk, banks are only making finance available where mergers are seen to make _____ for the industry.

9. Those interested in the takeover of Cadbury were _____, rather than private equity firms.

10. Deals like this one are seen as _____ with a greater likelihood of growth in the long term.

Prospects for the future

11. Banks and other financial institutions are likely to lend _____, in areas where risk can be managed more easily.

12. Mergers and acquisitions are likely to be funded by private _____ to a greater extent than they were before 2008.

7 Listen to the speech again and circle "True" or "False". Correct the false statements.

1. The speaker will say something of how he expects the future develops in the long term. True/False

2. The recession has changed the market for many businesses. True/False

3. The reasons of the mergers in financial sector differ from those of the mergers in other sectors. True/False

4. The speaker gives the example of Cadbury to illustrate how banks behave differently after 2008. True/False

5. There will be more speculative takeovers in the future though the banks will want to ensure that their loans get repaid. True/False

Business communication

TASK 8 Look at a travel website. Choose a destination and prepare a brief presentation on where to stay, what to do and where to eat there.

Useful language for presentations

Welcoming the audience

Good morning/afternoon, ladies and gentlemen.

Hello/Hi everyone.

It's a pleasure to welcome you today.

It's good to see you all here.

Introducing yourself

Let me introduce myself. I'm… from…

For those who don't know me, my name is…

As some of you know, I'm the purchasing manager.

Introducing your topic

What I'd like to present to you today is…

I'm here today to present…

The subject/topic of my presentation is…

Stating your purpose

The purpose of this presentation is to…

Our goal is to determine the best way to…

During the next few hours we'll be…

Outlining

My talk today consists of two parts. One is… and the other is…

I've divided my presentation into four parts.

I shall first talk about… and then touch on… and finally discuss…

Timing

My presentation will take about 30 minutes.

It will take about 20 minutes to cover these issues.

This won't take more than...

Questions

There will be time for questions after my presentation.

If you have any questions, feel free to interrupt me at any time.

Feel free to ask questions at any time during my talk.

Translation

 Translate the following sentences into Chinese.

1. Although imports from China in the same month reached £2.6 billion, the increase in exports came as good news to U.K. companies who had seen a reduction in their sales to the Asian giant in the preceding year.

   _____

   _____

2. Opportunities exist for an ever increasing number of U.K. companies, yet many fail as they do not put sufficient time and effort into understanding some fundamental differences between the two cultures.

   _____

   _____

3. An effective Chinese colleague will often be able to work out who in the other negotiating team holds real power, not always the boss, and help smooth out any possible problems.

   _____

   _____

4. Integrated channels offer the advantages of planning and control of resources, flow of information, and faster market penetration, and are a visible sign of commitment.

   _____

   _____

5. Most Western multinational corporations will realise that the huge markets of the developing countries are not for the products that they are selling at home, but for a far less sophisticated version at far less a price.

   _____

   _____

Translate the following sentences into English.

1. 消除进入壁垒是市场准入制度改革的必要环节，而市场准入制度是建立公平竞争市场过程中的重要机制。（essential）

   _____

2. 企业国际化始于对国际市场进入模式的选择，其发展过程也是企业不断进入新的国际市场和转换不同模式进入同一目标市场的过程。（evolve）

   _____

3. 2017 年上半年，在中国市场的拉动下，西班牙红酒出口额创历史新高，总额达到 13.207 亿欧元，比去年同期增长了 6%。（record high）

   _____

4. 进入新市场是企业家获取关键资源的重要途径，因为这一方式鼓励采用技术和最佳业务实践，而这两者是提高绩效的基础。（underlie）

   _____

5. 业务活动与其报酬大体相当，这意味着关联公司之间交易的条款、条件和定价应与独立第三方之间的交易相似。（transaction）

   _____

Writing

 Suppose you have received the following letter from a business acquaintance in China. Read the letter and write a reply.

> Floor 1A
> Beijing Commercial Centre
> 9 Chang Road, Beijing
> China
>
> 21 June 2011
>
> Dear
>
> I do not know if you remember me but we met at the RC Mandarin Hotel in Shanghai last month. You gave me your business card and kindly offered to help me if I ever planned to visit your country.

I am pleased to say I will be attending a trade fair in your city next month. I am in the process of making my travel arrangements and, as it is my first trip to your country, I would appreciate it if you could give me some advice.

In particular, I would welcome your advice on accommodation and how to get around the city. Should I arrange car hire, for example? Also, as I will have my evenings free, could you recommend places to eat? I will have a free day for sightseeing as well. What would you suggest I do?

I hope we can meet during my visit. I would very much like to invite you for a meal one evening if it is convenient.

Thank you again for your help. I hope to hear from you soon.

Regards

Chen Zhang

Business know-how

Read the following passage and figure out the plus and minus of taking M&A as a market entry mode.

Mergers and acquisitions（M&A 并购）

Mergers and acquisitions (M&A) are transactions in which the ownership of companies, other business organisations, or their operating units are transferred or consolidated with other entities. As an aspect of strategic management, M&A can allow enterprises to grow or downsize, and change the nature of their business or competitive position.

From a legal point of view, a merger is a legal consolidation of two entities into one entity, whereas an acquisition occurs when one entity takes ownership of another entity's stock, equity interests or assets. From a commercial and economic point of view, both types of transactions generally result in the consolidation of assets and liabilities under one entity, and the distinction between a "merger" and an "acquisition" is less clear. A transaction legally structured as an acquisition may have the effect of placing one party's business under the indirect ownership of the other party's shareholders, while a transaction legally structured as a merger may give each party's shareholders partial ownership and control of the combined enterprise. A deal may be euphemistically（委婉地）called a merger of equals if both CEOs agree that joining together is in the best interest of both of their companies, while when the deal is unfriendly (that is, when the management of the target company opposes the deal) it may be regarded as an "acquisition".

The rise of globalisation has exponentially（以指数方式）increased the necessity for agencies such as the Mergers and Acquisitions International Clearing (MAIC), trust accounts and securities clearing services for Like-Kind Exchanges for cross-border M&A.

Text B Business practices in China

Tanya Liddell, a successful exporter, shares his experiences with a local business association about doing business in China.

So, what is it like actually doing business with the Chinese? Well, it is difficult to describe because in China there's still no commonly shared perception of what's reasonable or normal in international business, so standards and expectations vary widely from place to place. That's why, when you're doing business in China, it is imperative that you do extensive preparatory work. This means finding out about the particular company, industry, city or region where you're doing business—and not just about the country as a whole.

One of the first things to remember is that the Chinese find it most discourteous if you are late for meetings. It may be, of course, that your first meeting will be in your hotel, but if not, then allow plenty of time for the journey as in most Chinese cities the congestion is every bit as bad as in London. A good tip is to take a business card with the company's address written in Chinese to show the taxi driver. When you get there, you will be greeted by your host, usually a senior manager, and probably some of his or her staff. The visitors will then be ushered into the meeting room.

The leader of your group will be expected to enter first and will generally be offered a seat beside the most senior Chinese person present.

This person will usually chair the meeting and act as host and have a translator at his or her side. To begin with, all those present will swap business cards, in itself a very important ceremony, and there will be a short period of small talk. The host will then officially start proceedings with a "brief introduction" to the Chinese enterprise and its activities. The host may then invite the visiting team to speak. Now at this point it is appropriate for the U.K. side to begin to make its case. Don't forget to warn your host beforehand if you wish to include any audiovisual aids during this presentation. It's also extremely important that your team should be able to answer any questions on any aspect of your business proposal, your own company and your international competitors.

Following the meeting, the Chinese enterprise will probably arrange a special dinner for the U.K. guests. Small talk over dinner is essential for relationship-building. For most Chinese, the family counts above all else. It remains the dominant social and political unit in Chinese society so Chinese people will usually be very pleased to be asked about their children and their hopes for their children's future. In social relationships Chinese people almost always seek to preserve harmony and face. Hosts believe it is their duty to offer their visitors hospitality, even though the visitors themselves may much prefer a day off after intense negotiations. It's very common, for instance, for the host enterprise to organise sightseeing trips for its guests and it would, of course, be a discourtesy not to accept these invitations.

Words and expressions

aid /eɪd/	n.	辅助	
audiovisual /ˌɔːdɪəʊˈvɪʒjuəl/	adj.	视听的	
ceremony /ˈserəməʊnɪ/	n.	仪式	
chair /tʃeə(r)/	v.	主持	
congestion /kənˈdʒestʃən/	n.	拥堵	
count /kaʊnt/	v.	有价值；被考虑	
discourteous /dɪsˈkɜːtɪəs/	adj.	失礼的	
discourtesy /dɪsˈkɜːtəsɪ/	n.	失礼	
hospitality /ˌhɒspɪˈtælətɪ/	n.	好客，殷勤	
imperative /ɪmˈperətɪv/	adj.	必要的	

preparatory /prɪˈpærətərɪ/	adj.	预备的	
preserve /prɪˈzɜːv/	v.	保存，保护	
swap /swɒp/	v.	交换	
vary /ˈveərɪ/	v.	变化；有不同	
every bit		完全	
make one's case		陈述意见	
sightseeing trip		观光旅行	
small talk		寒暄；闲谈	
usher into		迎入	

Comprehension tasks

 Read the text and complete the notes using up to three words or a number.

1. **On arrival in China** There are few universally accepted business norms in China as _____ vary throughout the country.

2. It is essential to do thorough _____ before visiting China.

3. It is viewed as extremely rude if you are _____ in China.

4. When travelling from your hotel, always take into account the severe _____ _____ in Chinese cities.

5. **Meetings** Upon arrival, you will normally be met by a _____ and fellow staff.

6. First of all, everyone exchanges _____ with one another.

7. The host will then formally open the meeting with a _____ _____ to the company and its operations.

8. Visitors should notify their hosts in advance if they intend to use _____ _____ .

9. **Socialising** Chinese hosts usually organise a _____ for foreign visitors.

10. A good topic of conversation is to enquire about your host's _____ _____ .

11. The Chinese feel an obligation to provide _____ at all times.

12. They will often arrange _____ for visitors.

 Read the text again and answer the following questions.

1. Why is it imperative to do extensive preparatory work when doing business in China?

2. Where do Chinese meet their foreign partners according to Tanya Liddell?

3. Who chairs the meeting usually?

4. What does "brief introduction" in the fourth paragraph mean?

5. Why is it a good topic to talk about the children of the Chinese business partners, according to Tanya Liddell?

Vocabulary

Put the following words or phrases into the correct group.

an arrangement	a mailshot	conversation	business
a joint venture	an investment	a partnership	a request
preparatory work	a commitment	a relationship	research

make	do	enter into
an arrangement		

Complete the sentences with the correct form of the following words.

| grow | restructure | merge | takeover |
| benefit | compete | streamline | acquire |

1. The telecoms sector was rocked when Vodafone launched a hostile _____ bid for Mannesmann.

2. After _____ with an Italian company, we had to re-assess our language training needs.

3. The chairman told shareholders that accepting the offer would lead to long-term _____ in sales.

4. The merger will help us to secure a _____ advantage over our biggest rivals.

5. There is no doubt that the merger will deliver substantial cost _____.

6. To fight a hostile bid, the company announced plans to _____ the workforce by cutting 2,000 jobs.

7. The move led to a major _____ programme, especially in duplicated areas such as administration.

8. After a period of major expansion through _____, we began to lose focus of our core activities.

TASK 5 Complete the following text by filling each gap with a suitable relative pronoun. Add any necessary commas.

The merger raises a number of HR issues (1) _____ will need to be addressed as a matter of urgency and in a manner (2) _____ is seen to be fair to the employees of both companies. Firstly the pay structures of the two companies (3) _____ show marked differences will need to be reviewed and harmonised. Furthermore redundancy terms will have to be agreed and offered to employees (4) _____ lose their jobs as a result of the merger. This is particularly important with regard to senior managers (5) _____ contracts contain severance clauses (6) _____ guarantee them generous terms. Our approach to these job cuts (7) _____ were promised to shareholders as part of the terms of the merger will also have a major effect on staff morale within the newly-formed company. It is imperative that we avoid any deterioration of staff morale (8) _____ could have an adverse effect on company performance.

Speaking

TASK 6 Choose one of the topics below and talk about it for one minute, using the framework below.

- how to research a new export market
- the importance of good preparation for a business trip

Opening sentence: _____
_____

Main points: Supporting ideas:
- _____   - _____
- _____   - _____
- _____   - _____

Concluding sentence: _____

TASK 7 Form a pair and discuss the following topic.

What advice would you give to the people visiting your country on business?

Business communication

 Make a 3-minute presentation to introduce a recent merger. Include information about its size, products and markets.

Useful language developing the speech

Announcing the beginning of the speech

To begin with, I would like to talk about a principle.

I think it would be best to start out by looking at some pictures.

Shifting to the next main point

Well, let's move on to the next point.

We will now come to the second problem.

Next, I would like to turn to a more difficult problem.

The next point I'd like to talk about is the feasibility of this project.

That brings me to my second point.

Introducing the supporting materials

Please allow me to deal with this matter more extensively.

I'll expand this topic with drawings and figures.

I will not go into detail on it.

Expressions concerning audio visual aids

I apologise that this slide is not so clear, but I hope you can still make out the general idea.

Sorry for the small print.

I'm sorry we left a figure out here.

Explaining the contents on the slides

This slide demonstrates…

On this slide, you can see…

This curve in this slide shows…

This figure in this slide exhibits…

This table on this slide presents…

This diagram on this slide depicts…

This chart on this slide displaces…

The picture on this slide shows…

TASK 9 Translate the following sentences into Chinese.

1. It is difficult to describe because in China there's still no commonly shared perception of what's reasonable or normal in international business, so standards and expectations vary widely from place to place.

2. It may be, of course, that your first meeting will be in your hotel, but if not, then allow plenty of time for the journey as in most Chinese cities the congestion is every bit as bad as in London.

3. It remains the dominant social and political unit in Chinese society so Chinese people will usually be very pleased to be asked about their children and their hopes for their children's future.

4. In China, talking too much can come across as arrogant, discourteous and even rude and, whilst it may not be apparent at the time, it's likely to cut things off before they've even got started!

5. Social etiquette and behavioural norms help to preserve a harmonious environment in which a person's face—along with their social standing and reputation can be upheld.

TASK 10 Translate the following sentences into English.

1. 就像世界各地说英语的人一样，中国人也经常用闲聊来开始交谈，这样可以打破僵局，有助于在进入正题之前建立人际关系。(small talk)

2. 这里的居民热情好客，无论在什么情况下，只要你有事相求，他们都会热情相助。甚至对素不相识的陌生人也会以笑脸相迎。(hospitality)

3. 移动技术在中国迅速发展，特别是在消费者服务领域。因此我们的团队相信，这一趋势将为日常生活带来深远的、根本性的改善。(usher in)

_____

_____

4. 剪彩仪式让企业主或经理有机会简单介绍自己的业务，并公开感谢他们的财务支持方、员工、他们的朋友和家人，以及他们的商业伙伴。(ceremony)

_____

_____

5. 筹备会议的目的是邀请理事会成员对中国南亚商业论坛的两个重要问题进行头脑风暴，该论坛将于今年 6 月在中国举行。(preparatory)

_____

_____

Writing

TASK 11 Suppose a foreign business associate is visiting your company for three days. You have been asked to organise the visit and plan appropriate entertainment. Write a letter to the visitor outlining a timetable for the visit and describing the activities you have planned.

UNIT **4** Trade fair

Warming up

 What are the benefits of trade fairs for exhibitors and visitors? Discuss it with your partner.

 Here is a list of trade fair slogans. Which one do you like best? Give your reasons.

1. Always Know Who You're Talking To.
2. All Parts Working Together.
3. Give Us a Try.
4. Let's Work Together.
5. No Ordinary Company.
6. We Work Best When We Work with You.
7. The Recipe for Success.
8. We Won't Leave You Hanging.
9. We're Here for You.
10. The Revolution Is Here.

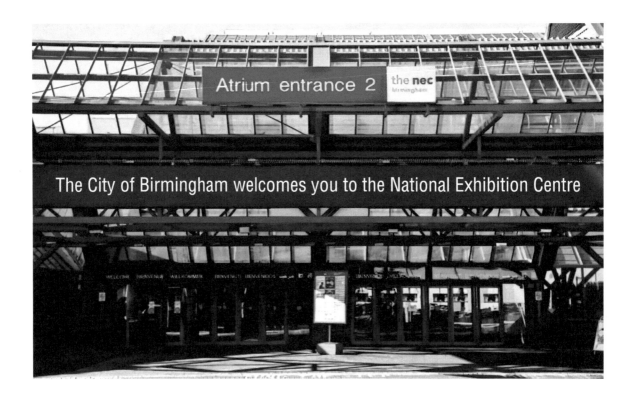

Can you afford to miss this year's Festival of Ceramics?

28th–29th October 2011 • The NEC Birmingham
Friday&Saturday 09:30–17:30

The Festival of Ceramics is the leading ceramics event in Europe, with a growing following from Asia. Celebrating its twenty-third year, this is the event for companies to showcase their creative designs to a worldwide audience of buyers.

This year over 400 companies will be in Birmingham to display their new products. For buyers this offers a unique opportunity to see the full range on offer in the ceramic community today and to meet the people responsible for providing the designs of the future.

Each company that attends the show has been selected to ensure that you, the buyer, will be able to see products which are both practical and inspirational. Whether you are interested in specialist, highly individual ceramic pieces or more practical, mainstream products this is the show to keep you ahead of the competition.

The exhibition at the NEC attracts 30,000 U.K. and international quality buyers, suppliers and professionals from across the world who attend to see what new, interesting products are on offer and to network, develop and expand within the consistently growing creative ceramics industry.

More than fifty exhibitors will be attending The Festival of Ceramics for the first time this year, giving buyers a unique chance to meet the people who will be making tomorrow's headlines.

Show features include:

- **FREE** Workshops featuring the latest products.
- **FREE** Business Seminars highlighting current topics.
- *Leading Pavilion* showcasing new designers.

Words and expressions

audience	/ˈɔːdɪəns/	n.	观众；听众；爱好者	pavilion	/pəˈvɪljən/	n. 展示馆；亭子
ceramic	/sɪˈræmɪk/	n.	陶瓷制品	showcase	/ˈʃəʊkeɪs/	v. 展示，陈列
consistently	/kənˈsɪstəntlɪ/	adv.	一贯地	specialist	/ˈspeʃəlɪst/	n. 专家
feature	/ˈfiːtʃə(r)/	v.	以……为特色	unique	/juːˈniːk/	adj. 独特的；极好的
headline	/ˈhedlaɪn/	n.	头版头条新闻	on offer		供出售的
inspirational	/ˌɪnspəˈreɪʃənəl/	adj.	鼓舞人心的；给予灵感的			

Comprehension tasks

TASK 1 Read the text and complete the following table.

The exhibition	It is called (1) _____. It exhibits both highly individual ceramic pieces and (2) _____ products. The (3) _____ exhibition takes place at the NEC in Birmingham (4) _____. There are also (5) _____ and a showcase for new designers.
The exhibitors	Over (6) _____ exhibitors are selected to display (7) _____. More than fifty places are kept for (8) _____.
The visitors	Each exhibition attracts about (9) _____ U.K. and international (10) _____.

 Read the text again and judge whether the following sentence are "True", "False" or "Not given".

1. The exhibition is not open at the weekend. _____

2. Ceramic manufacturers, designers, and buyers will come to the exhibition from different parts of the world. _____

3. The latest ceramic products will be displayed at the business seminars. _____

4. The visitors can get registered online at the official website of the exhibition. _____

5. The buyers will get an opportunity to meet some well-known people in Europe. _____

Vocabulary

Use the clues below to find the nine trade fair words in the puzzle.

E	X	H	I	B	I	T	I	O	N
B	D	O	T	I	W	E	T	M	E
R	G	I	F	T	S	S	I	A	X
O	E	R	S	E	R	A	C	I	H
C	S	A	M	P	L	E	K	L	I
H	T	H	H	T	L	R	E	O	B
U	A	F	A	A	R	A	T	R	I
R	N	B	R	L	E	T	Y	D	T
E	D	O	T	D	L	Y	O	E	O
W	O	R	K	S	H	O	P	R	R

1. an event where things are shown to the public (exhibition)
2. a thin glossy booklet giving product information
3. things which are given free to customers to promote a product
4. a temporary display area that a company constructs at an exhibition
5. service allowing customers to purchase products by post
6. a meeting where people learn by discussing experiences and doing practical activities
7. something you need to attend an exhibition
8. a small example of a product to show what it is like
9. a person who displays something at an exhibition

Complete each sentence with an appropriate word the first letter of which is given.

1. Organisers can promote an exhibition by placing an a_____ in a newspaper or magazine.
2. Exhibition organisers often respond to enquiries with a standard letter of t_____.
3. Companies interested in exhibiting have to complete an a_____ form and send samples.
4. The d_____ of the stand and publicity material needs to fit in with our corporate image.
5. Earls Court hosts many top international e_____ throughout the year.
6. One of the main b_____ for exhibitors is the chance to meet customers face to face.

7. Exhibition organisers often reserve a number of s_____ for first-time exhibitors.

8. Buyers come from independent r_____ as well as large department stores.

9. At an exhibition, visitors can see the actual goods rather than just photos in b_____.

TASK 5 Re-arrange the words to make formal phrases or expressions from written correspondence.

1. enclosed / please / find

    _____

2. letter / of / to / reference / with / your

    _____

3. look / meeting / we / forward / to / you

    _____

4. to / our / conversation / further / of

    _____

5. further / questions / should / have / you / any

    _____

6. not / do / please / me / hesitate / contact / to

    _____

Listening and speaking

TASK 6 Listen to a conversation and fill in the blanks with the missing information.

Jan:	Hi Ross, it's Jan. I hear you are going to the trade fair in Poznan next week.
Ross:	Yes. ¹_____?
Jan:	No, I'm not. But Monica's asked me to give you some details about travel arrangements and so on.
Ross:	Oh right, great.
Jan:	Do you have a pen ready?
Ross:	Sure, ²_____.
Jan:	Right. Your plane lands at Poznan at 10:20 on Thursday. It's flight BA442. When you get there, ³_____ at the airport by Sergiusz Jablonski.
Ross:	Will I be going into meetings as soon as I arrive or am I going to the hotel first?
Jan:	Sergiusz is taking you to your hotel. Once ⁴_____, he'll take you to lunch with some of the managers.

Ross: OK. Is there anything planned for the evening?

Jan: ⁵_____, but they haven't sent us any details. I'm sure Sergiusz will let you know what's going on when you get there.

Ross: OK. Let's see now. Is there anything else I need to know before I go?

Jan: ⁶_____. Your return flight's at 11:55 the next morning, so you'll have plenty of time to have a relaxed breakfast and ⁷_____ to the airport in good time.

7 Work in pairs to make up a conversation between Ross and Sergiusz Jablonski at Poznan airport.

Business communication

8 Suppose you work for a ceramic manufacturer in China, and you have learned about the trade fair held in Birmingham. Hold a meeting with your partner to discuss whether you should apply for attendance or not.

Translation

9 Translate the following sentences into Chinese.

1. Celebrating its twenty-third year, this is the event for companies to showcase their creative designs to a worldwide audience of buyers.

   _____

   _____

2. For buyers this offers a unique opportunity to see the full range on offer in the ceramic community today and to meet the people responsible for providing the designs of the future.

   _____

   _____

3. The exhibition at the NEC attracts 30,000 U.K. and international quality buyers, suppliers and professionals from across the world who attend to see what new, interesting products are on offer and to network, develop and expand within the consistently growing creative ceramics industry.

   _____

   _____

4. Local government units, businesses, and small and medium-sized enterprises will feature their products and services in a trade fair during the Spring Festival Shopping Week.

_____

5. To celebrate International Women's Day (March 8) the U.K.'s leading fair trade organisation has been highlighting the inspirational role of one of its team who is helping thousands of families to work their way out of poverty.

_____

_____

TASK 10 **Translate the following sentences into English.**

1. 目前，外贸中心经营管理着广州市最大的两个展馆——中国出口商品交易会琶洲展馆和流花路展馆，两馆室内展厅面积总和达 25 万平方米。(pavilion)

_____

_____

2. 我们预期无论是在主流产品还是奢侈品领域，都将有不同的高品质参展商纷纷亮相于本交易会的首秀，这同时也是一块获得高规格赞助机会的敲门砖。(mainstream)

_____

_____

3. 该展会重点展示智能装备、新型传感器、3D 打印等龙头企业的主导产品，以及企业产品数据化、营销服务网络化、生产线无人化管理、渠道经销商网络化等成果。(showcase)

_____

_____

4. 该公司秉持匠心理念，运用多元化现代工艺，打造出更加时尚、实用的银质餐器、茶器等产品，为消费者带来更好的生活美学体验。(practical)

_____

_____

5. 你要意识到不断变化的贸易趋势，并用足够的灵活性加以应对和利用，才能跟上竞争对手的步伐并保持领先地位。(keep... ahead of...)

_____

_____

Suppose your company received an enquiry and you are expected to write a letter of reply. Give details about the company's products/services and prices. Consider the following.

- who the reader is and what information is needed
- the purpose, order and content of paragraphs
- your main points and supporting ideas in each paragraph

Business know-how

Read the following passage about counterfeiting and discuss with your partner what effective measures can be taken against this problem.

Counterfeiting（伪造；仿造）

To counterfeit means to imitate something. Counterfeit products are fakes（假货；赝品）or unauthorised replicas（仿制品）of the real product. Counterfeit products are often produced with the intent to take advantage of the superior value of the imitated product. The word counterfeit frequently describes both the forgeries（伪造品）of currency and documents, as well as the imitations of items such as clothing, handbags, shoes, pharmaceuticals, aviation and automobile parts, watches, electronics (both parts and finished products), software, works of art, toys, and movies.

Counterfeit products tend to have fake company logos and brands (resulting in patent or trademark infringement (侵犯，侵害) in the case of goods), have a reputation for being lower quality (sometimes not working at all) and may even include toxic elements such as lead. This has resulted in the deaths of hundreds of thousands of people, due to automobile and aviation accidents, poisoning, or ceasing to take essential compounds (e.g., in the case a person takes non-working medicine).

Text B Replying to enquiries about an exhibition

The following is a letter of reply to enquiries about an exhibition.

28th–29th October 2011
The NEC Birmingham

Dear

Thank you for your interest in the 2011 Festival of Ceramics show. As requested, I enclose full details of this and future shows for you.

Held in Birmingham the Festival of Ceramics attracts buyers who understand the importance of good design and practical products. The Festival allows you to meet customers, old and new, face to face, in an atmosphere that allows you to show your products to their best advantage.

Now in its twenty-third year, the Festival of Ceramics remains the largest U.K.-based exhibition for ceramics. From the smallest egg cups to the largest pots for the garden, all can be found here at this exciting exhibition. So, whatever your ceramic products there will be a place for them. The exhibition has been attracting over 30,000 U.K. and overseas buyers since it moved to the NEC three years ago. Buyers who attend come from independent retailers, department stores, mail-order houses and Internet traders. If these are the people you need to meet, you will not be disappointed.

The key to the continuing popularity of the Festival of Ceramics is its selection of exhibitors, ensuring that buyers are seeing the very best in the industry. In addition to workshops, business seminars and shows, we give support to people in the industry, enabling them to make the right decisions.

Festival of Ceramics is always oversubscribed and by the time this letter reaches you, many of the available stands will already have been rebooked. Therefore, we recommend you reserve your stand as soon as possible and we guarantee all applications will be given our full attention the moment we receive them.

If you require any further information or advice, please do not hesitate to call Alex Whittle or myself on 0118 9784332 or email us on info@festivalofceramics.com.

I look forward to hearing from you.

Best wishes

Liz Copping

Liz Copping
Sales Manager

Words and expressions

atmosphere /'ætməsfɪə(r)/	*n.* 氛围		**stand** /stænd/	*n.* 展台	
enable /ɪ'neɪbl/	*v.* 使能够		**egg cup**	蛋杯	
oversubscribe /ˌəʊvəsəb'skraɪb/	*v.* 过量预定		**in addition to**	除……以外	
popularity /ˌpɒpju'lærətɪ/	*n.* 流行；广受欢迎		**Internet trader**	网商	
pot /pɒt/	*n.* 壶；盆；罐		**to one's advantage**	对某人有利	

Comprehension tasks

 Read the letter and find examples of the following.

standard letter phrases   main points

organisation of letters

supporting ideas   linking words

 Read the text again and answer the following questions.

1. What is the purpose of the Festival of Ceramics?
2. What kind of people does the Festival of Ceramics tend to attract?
3. What is the key to the success of the Festival of Ceramics?
4. What is the purpose of the letter?

Vocabulary

 Complete the following information with phrases from the Festival of Ceramics letter.

 **Don't forget**

Standard letter phrases

The following phrases are useful when writing letters.

- **Referring to an earlier letter or conversation**
  With reference to your letter dated... in which...
  Further to our conversation of...

  _____

- **Enclosing**
  Please find enclosed...

  _____

- **Offering assistance**
  Should you have any further questions, please contact me on...

  _____

- **Referring to future contact**
  We look forward to meeting you on...

  _____

Some of the following lines contain an unnecessary word. If a line is correct, write CORRECT. If there is an extra word in the line, write the extra word in CAPITAL LETTERS.

1. With a reference to your letter dated 13 November, _____
2. in which you requested information about our _____
3. forthcoming exhibition "Management in Action", _____
4. please do find enclosed details about this and _____
5. future events in the region. "Management in Action" _____
6. which is the showcase event for the region's major _____
7. business training organisations. This year's exhibition _____
8. it includes 30 free taster workshops, covering _____
9. these areas such as motivation, health and safety, _____
10. team-building, presentation skills and e-commerce. _____
11. If you require any further information, and please _____
12. do not hesitate to contact either myself or Elizabeth _____
13. Wellington on 01952 345642. We are look forward to _____
14. hearing from you in the near future. _____

Match the words and then use them to complete the sentences below.

long-term ——— interests
independent ——— commitment
trade   retailers
commercial   negotiations
entry   strategy
intense   literature

1. Doing business overseas is a <u>long-term commitment</u> not a way of making quick profits.
2. Do you have any _____ on the product I could take away and read?
3. After several weeks of _____, we finally reached an agreement on price.
4. We don't have our own shops. We sell directly to local _____.
5. Our _____ for getting into the U.S. was to find a joint venture partner.
6. It's a prestigious event and very much in our _____ to exhibit at it.

Speaking

 6 Suppose your company wishes to exhibit at a trade fair. Discuss and decide the following.

- your objectives for the trade fair
- where and when you should exhibit

 7 Form a pair and discuss the following topic with your partner.

Have you ever been to a trade fair? If yes, what impressed you most there?

Business communication

 8 Discuss with your partner about what should be done to get ready for the trade fair in detail. You may consider the following.

- Inviting clients
- Preparing samples
- Preparing for negotiations
- Promotional materials

TASK 9 Translate the following sentences into Chinese.

1. The Festival allows you to meet customers, old and new, face to face, in an atmosphere that allows you to show your products to their best advantage.

   _____

   _____

2. Festival of Ceramics is always oversubscribed and by the time this letter reaches you, many of the available stands will already have been rebooked. Therefore, we recommend you reserve your stand as soon as possible and we guarantee all applications will be given our full attention the moment we receive them.

   _____

   _____

3. Exhibitions assemble the same product in different industries or different products in the same industry, providing the public with the opportunity to choose and compare while saving a lot of time and cost for the organisation's publicity and promotion.

   _____

   _____

4. According to the prediction of insiders, in the next three years, the exhibition market in China will call for 2 million employees, including approximately 500,000 senior exhibition managers, and the numbers will increase by an annual rate of 15%.

   _____

   _____

5. Since it is an inevitable trend for China to open its market to foreign exhibition industry, how to coordinate the relationship between national exhibition industry and international exhibition industry becomes an issue that must be carefully considered in the policy making process.

   _____

   _____

TASK 10 Translate the following sentences into English.

1. 尽管 Medjool Village Dates 的主要出口市场是欧洲和中东，该公司目前依然期望在不久的将来能打入亚洲市场。(look forward to)

   _____

   _____

2. 报价时要坚定、果断、毫不犹豫，这样才能显示出报价者的信心，并给对方留下认真而诚实的好印象。（hesitate）

_____

_____

3. 在 2017 北京国际服务贸易交易会现场，一些传统文化非遗展台吸引了参会人员的关注。（stand）

_____

_____

4. 感谢贵公司 8 月 13 日的来信及随附的邀请函，我公司很荣幸地接受贵方的邀请参加定于 10 月 15 日至 10 月 20 日在上海举办的商品交易会。（enclose）

_____

_____

5. 判断一个展会是否成功，除了看展位展出效果以外，配套市场宣传活动的质量也是必不可少的衡量标准。（in addition to）

_____

_____

Writing

Suppose you work for Meridian Promotions, an exhibition organiser. You have been asked to reply to the enquiry below. Use the following phrases and handwritten notes to write a formal letter.

please do not hesitate to	we look forward to hearing from you
we are pleased to confirm that	please find enclosed
should you have any questions	with reference to

DS

Defrag Software
Mozartplein 44
1042 Amsterdam
The Netherlands

The Bookings Officer
Meridian Promotions
24 Spring Gardens
London W2

12 July 2011

Re: Futuresoft International 2012

Dear Sir/Madam

- Thank him for the enquiry
- Dates for 2012: 24–26 October
- Enclose booking form and floor plan with available places

I am writing to enquire about next year's Futuresoft exhibition. We are a new but fast-growing software developer based in Amsterdam who would be very interested in displaying at the Futuresoft International Exhibition 2012.

We would be very grateful if you could confirm the dates for next year's exhibition and whether there is still exhibition space available. If this is the case, could you please send details of available spots, their prices and a booking form?

As we have not previously exhibited at Futuresoft, we would also be very grateful for any other information about exhibiting, in particular guidelines on display stands and the availability of power, etc.

I look forward to hearing from you soon.

Best regards

Arnold van Rijn
Managing Director
Defrag Software

- Application must be in by 1 September and full payment by 1 October
- Enclose display stand guidelines
- Ask him to submit product information and details of their display stand

Review Test 1

TASK 1 Listen to the recording and for each question, mark one letter a, b or c.

1. Why did Jan give Ross a call?

   a. To give Ross some information about her travel arrangements.

   b. To ask Ross to go to the trade fair in Poznan next week.

   c. To book an air ticket for her.

   d. To give her details about the trade fair.

2. Which of the following information about Ross's flight is correct?

   a. It will take off from Poznan at 10:30 on Thursday.

   b. It will arrive in Poznan at 10:20 on Thursday.

   c. It will take off from Poznan at 10:20 on Tuesday.

   d. It will arrive in Poznan at 10:20 on Tuesday.

3. What will Ross do firstly after she leaves the airport?

   a. Meet Sergiusz Jablonski.

   b. Meet some of the managers.

   c. Check in at the hotel.

   d. Have lunch.

4. What does Jan say about the evening plan?

   a. She doesn't think there is going to be anything planned for the evening.

   b. She imagines some details for the evening plan.

   c. She believes that Sergiusz will arrange for the evening plan.

   d. She hasn't got any information about the evening plan yet.

5. What else does Ross need to know before she leaves for the trade fair, according to Jan?

   a. She has plenty of time to have a relaxing breakfast.

   b. Get up early to catch the plane.

   c. Her return ticket is at 11:55 the next morning so she doesn't need to hurry.

   d. Nothing else.

TASK 2 Listen to an interview and fill in the blanks.

1. We have had a reasonable degree of _____ in retirement age for a long time now.

2. So, in one sense, these changes are likely to _____.

3. Those who wish to retire will. Where it affects businesses is in the administration of people's retirement, and in cases where an employee wants to _____, but the employer thinks

otherwise.

4. So it is only in a _____ that someone will want to continue working, but the company would prefer for them not to.

5. We already have an aging working population, and _____ are not getting the opportunities in their careers.

TASK 3 Listen to a report and answer the following questions.

1. How much did Geely pay for Volvo?

_____

2. How profitable is Volvo?

_____

3. How did Chinese markets respond to the deal?

_____

Part II   Reading and writing

TASK 4 Read the following passage and choose the correct answer for each blank from a, b, c and d.

Ken Towle, chief executive of Tesco China, announced the retailer planned to open over a hundred new hypermarkets and 50 "Lifespace" malls. The (1) _____ will double the number of hypermarkets Tesco has in China to over 200 and triple the number of customers its stores receive per week to 12 million.

Tesco currently has 82 hypermarkets and four 500,000 sq ft shopping malls stretching (2) _____ eastern China. The "Lifespace" mall concept has the Tesco hypermarket as its anchor store but incorporates other shops, restaurants and family entertainment and the company claims that footfall at its existing malls is around 600,000 customers a week. Tesco already has more (3) _____ selling space abroad than in Britain but its overseas business, which includes loss-making start-ups in China and the U.S.A., produces a third of sales and a fifth of group profits.

Tesco and their foreign competitors such as Wal-Mart, Carrefour and Metro are expanding rapidly in emerging markets to (4) _____ sluggish growth at home. The rewards in China are enticing with grocery sales expected to hit £600 bn this year and 1,200 supermarkets and hypermarkets to open by 2014. Tesco said China offered an "unrivalled opportunity in a large, rapidly growing market"—221 cities are (5) _____ to have more than one million inhabitants by 2025, while Europe currently has only 35 cities in this category.

1.	a. movement	b. move	c. moving	d. touch
2.	a. of	b. in	c. along	d. away
3.	a. chips and mortar	b. bricks and motor	c. bricks and mortar	d. chips
4.	a. make out	b. make up for	c. make up	d. make of
5.	a. predicted	b. predicting	c. predict	d. prediction

 Read the graphs below and choose the best answer from a, b, c and d.

Question 1 is based on the following graph.

The graph shows the price for Tesco shares over a three-month period.

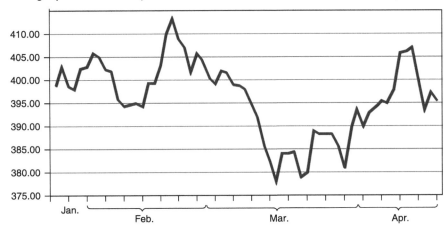

1. Which of the following statements is NOT true?

   a. There were some fluctuations in the Tesco share price from January to April.

   b. The Tesco price reached a high towards the end of February.

   c. By the middle of March the Tesco share price had fallen to a low of 378.

   d. In April, it rose slightly, before settling back to around the 395 that it is today.

Questions 2–3 are based on the following graph.

Look at the share prices of Marks and Spencer and The Carphone Warehouse over a six-month period.

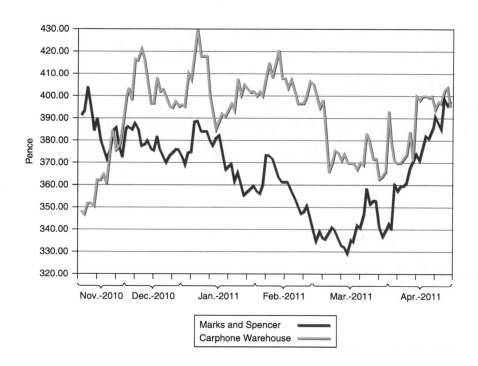

2. When did the share prices of both Marks and Spencer and The Carphone Warehouse reach about 380p?

3. Which of the following statements is NOT true?

   a. Whilst M&S shares had fallen from 400p, those of CW's had risen from an earlier low of 350p.

   b. Both fell slowly over the next few months, although CW's were more volatile, and showed some signs of recovery, only to dip again.

   c. Both reached their low at about the same time, with M&S's falling to 330p, and CW's being approximately 30 points higher.

   d. They generally remained stable at the 400p mark throughout March.

Questions 4–5 are based on the following graph.

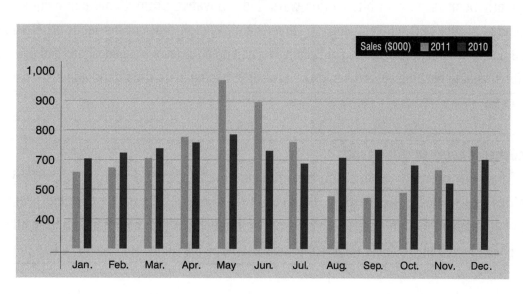

4. When did the company's sales peak in the year of 2011?

    a. January   **b.** March   **c.** May   **d.** December

5. Which of the following is true according to the graph?

    a. Sales had a quick start in 2011 compared to 2010.

    b. The general point about sales in 2011 fluctuated a lot more than in 2010.

    c. In 2011, sales collapsed in summer a lot worse than 2010.

    d. Sales finished poorly in 2011.

 Read the following two passages. Choose the best answer to each question.

Questions 1–5 are based on Passage 1.

Passage 1

A

> **Michael Martins, *Chairman, Ecofoodsmart***
>
> Michael Martins has recently returned to Ecofoodsmart, the large retail food chain, after a 20-year absence. Whilst away, he held a variety of posts in local government including that of mayor for six years, where his skills as an effective public speaker won him great respect. He then returned to the industry as one of the two architects behind the dramatic revival of the Remco supermarket chain. His comprehensive and varied experience of the retail food sector will make a huge impact on Ecofoodsmart and he has already embarked on an ambitious policy of major acquisitions.

B

> **Steven Waugh, *Chief Executive Officer, DigiCom***
>
> Steven Waugh, the driving force behind DigiCom for over 25 years, retires this year. Known for his quick decision-making, he is seen as one of the most outspoken and ruthless operators in the world of business. These qualities have often made life difficult for DigiCom competitors, who have regularly been faced with bitter price wars and innovative promotional campaigns, often masterminded by the CEO himself. Born in Queensland, Waugh first cut his teeth on Australia's Channel 9 before entering broadcasting in Britain. Never a great believer in political correctness, he is famous for spending his time aboard his luxury cruiser indulging in gourmet food and champagne.

C

> **Mark Boucher, *Chairman, Gladstone***
>
> Mark Boucher, 53, chairs Gladstone, the base-metals group recently demerged from Corgen of South Africa and floated in Amsterdam. Since the breakaway, Gladstone's operating profit has grown to $92 m, even though experts have described the company as overstaffed and inefficient. Boucher is a reserved man who is reluctant to address large meetings but reveals, when pressed,

a dry sense of humour. He has had an unusual career path, including a spell working for the North American Space Agency, followed by a stint running a satellite TV station.

D

Erik Johanssen, *Chief Executive, MorgenReynolds*

MorgenReynolds' CEO Erik Johanssen admits to crying occasionally and says he is not the tough hard-nosed businessman that people expect when they meet him. He is, however, universally regarded as a shrewd politician within the industry. A self-styled company man, the chain smoking 55 year-old Johanssen has been with Morgen for over 20 years. Since Morgen took over the innovative but underperforming Reynolds, Johanssen has streamlined the business radically, axing half of Reynolds' top managers. Johanssen lives modestly in Stockholm and travels to work by underground.

E

Joe Anderson, *Chief Executive, Dayton International Hotels*

Joe Anderson joined the imaginative Seattle-based Foyles restaurant chain after graduating in 1973. He worked his way up through the ranks, performing a variety of different roles, eventually becoming the Managing Director in 1986 and joining the parent company's executive board in 1990. In 2004 he became CEO and President of the group's Dayton International Hotels division. Anderson has focused on Dayton's core restaurant and hotel activities and reduced the group's debts by disposing of several properties and a chain of beauty salons. His next project is likely to be the search for strategic alliances with major European hotel chains.

Read the sentences below and the profiles of the five international executives above. Who does each sentence below refer to? For each sentence, mark one letter A, B, C, D or E.

1. He has cut operating costs by reducing the number of senior staff.
2. He does not enjoy making presentations and speeches.
3. He started his career working for a television station.
4. He improved the company's financial position by selling off assets.
5. He is expanding the company with a series of takeovers.

Questions 6–10 are based on Passage 2.

Passage 2

NewStart, the European online recruiter, announced this week that it was to shut down all U.K. operations, raising doubts about the future profitability of the online recruitment sector. The Dutch-owned company is to cut 525 jobs from its 876 strong workforce and concentrate on its markets in the Netherlands, Germany and Belgium.

6. _____. Despite such healthy brand recognition and its website carrying 14,000 vacancies, mounting losses have forced the company into liquidation.

7. _____. The losses are large for a company rapidly running out of cash. Like many other companies, NewStart expanded aggressively and burnt through shareholder capital far more quickly than its business model was able to generate profits. In the six months to September, cash reserves fell from £30 m to just £14 m. The company's shares have fallen just as dramatically, from €62 in March to just €0.3 at the time of the announcement.

8. _____. However, online job hunting is clearly here to stay with web recruitment being such an ideal application of Internet technology. Jobhunters can search through thousands of vacancies quickly and efficiently and they can register CVs for the attention of thousands of companies at a fraction of the cost of posting them individually. There are over one million vacancies on the Internet in the U.K. at the moment. The problem is that there are also well over a thousand recruitment websites. There doesn't seem to be much doubt that the industry will survive but NewStart is unlikely to be the last to go under.

Online recruitment is still a growing market but dozens of companies like NewStart fail every year, facing fierce competition from established players such as Monster Worldwide, the U.K.'s largest online recruiter, which employs over 4,000 people in 36 countries. More and more companies now see the Internet as vital to their recruitment strategy; an ever-growing number of companies don't just advertise online but are making online application the only option available to would-be new recruits.

9. _____. There will be times when companies don't want their competitors to know that they're looking to replace a key executive. Some sensitive hirings can only be done by a headhunter so the internet has its obvious limitations. There is also the issue of security. There have been notable cases recently where it came to light that applicants had to submit personal information and credit card numbers through a non-secure website. Such headlines will only confirm many people's natural distrust of the Internet.

Whether the growth in online recruitment will be enough to tempt investors back to companies like NewStart remains to be seen. New Chief Executive Ray Arnold is hoping to raise fresh finance.

10. _____

_____.

Choose one of the following phrases or sentences marked a to e to fill in the blanks above numbered 6 to 10.

a. Shareholders, meanwhile, are very aware that business is currently down and are waiting for more information soon.

b. With the collapse of NewStart's market value, investors are questioning whether there is still money to be made from internet recruitment.

c. However, online recruitment isn't suitable for every vacancy.

d. One of the most widely-known brands in the industry, NewStart was famous for its €6m sponsorship of televised sport in the U.K.

e. NewStart announced third quarter losses of £10m, down from £25m the previous quarter.

Suppose you have been asked to write a report on your company's staffing requirements. Use the information below to write a report. Consider your reader and purpose and use an appropriate level of formality. Include the following information.

- the number of new people each department needs
- the kind of candidates that are needed
- how these people should be recruited

---

email	RE: Staff requirements

From:	Barthez, Alex [abarthez@castorceramics.com]
Sent:	Thursday 18 February 12:51 p.m.
To:	Lambert, Jasmin
Subject:	RE: Staff requirements

Jasmin

Thanks for your email yesterday. I was going to speak to you about taking on another sales rep this year anyway. All this reorganising of the sales team means we need someone for the Mediterranean markets. Better get someone with loads of experience as it's going to be tricky setting up a new office there. We're hoping to open the office in about 6 months, so we'd better start looking soon.

All the best.

Alex

Jasmin

You wanted to know about staffing levels in production. Well, I reckon we'll need another five people for holiday cover this summer. George is retiring next year so it might be an idea to keep a couple of them on afterwards even.

Javagal

Jasmin

Thanks for the note about secretarial resourcing. If you ask me, I think we'll need to look at a couple of new people. Martha is going on maternity leave soon and we don't know yet whether she's coming back afterwards. And there's always holidays, of course. Could we advertise for two new secretarial staff? If we advertise locally, it'll be cheap and then we can train them up.

Louise

Briefly define the following underlined business terms in English and translate each term into Chinese.

1. The food of <u>entrepreneurship</u> is capital.
   Definition: _____
   Translation: _____

2. <u>Human resources management</u> has a large demand as well as the supply.
   Definition: _____
   Translation: _____

3. Organic growth through <u>mergers and acquisitions</u> will not bring companies effective profit growths in the short term.
   Definition: _____
   Translation: _____

4. It is a crime to <u>counterfeit</u> money.
   Definition: _____
   Translation: _____

5. <u>Headhunting</u> is on the increase as advertising becomes less and less cost-effective.
   Definition: _____
   Translation: _____

 Translate the following Chinese paragraph into English.

任何怀疑中国航空公司雄心的人，只需看看大兴国际机场的计划就行了。大兴国际机场将于 2019 年 9 月底投入运营。它将是世界上最大的机场，拥有 8 条跑道和每年达 1 亿乘客的吞吐量。这些新设施是为了满足快速增长的航空旅行需求而建设的。

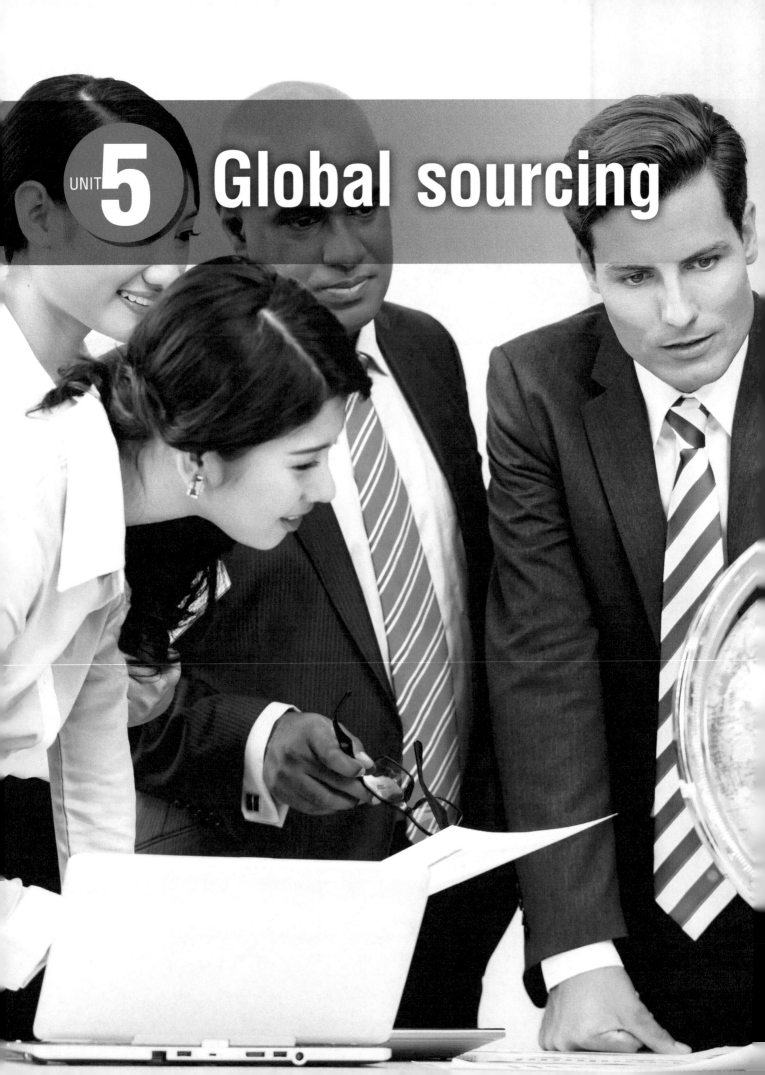

UNIT 5 Global sourcing

Warming up

 What type of suppliers may a company use? What criteria should a company apply when choosing suppliers?

 Companies tend to consider four main criteria when choosing a supplier. Complete the table below with the following measurements.

Percent defective	$ per unit
Satisfaction surveys	Number of new product launches a year
Time to market	Total number of days late
Warranty dollars spent	Number of items in the catalogue

Main criteria when choosing a supplier		
Criteria	**Definitions**	**Measurements**
Cost	Cost relative to our competitors	
Quality	Conformance to standards	*Percent defective*
	Performance	
	Reliability	
Delivery	Speed	
	Reliability	
Flexibility	Product range	
	New product introduction	

Text A Supplier relationships

Craig Barksdale works as a consultant at Jefferson Watson. He talks about different types of supplier relationship.

I = Interviewer **C** = Craig

I We keep hearing all about the globalisation of markets and supply chains and so on but why has global sourcing suddenly become so widespread?

C Well, I think there are several factors, really. I mean, as companies expand internationally their outlook becomes increasingly global. What's more, hyper-competitive domestic markets have driven companies to look further afield in their search for competitive advantage. Although I think the process has really been accelerated by rapid advances in IT and telecoms. That's been the real catalyst for change.

I And what's the great attraction? Why are companies so keen to source abroad?

C It depends on the circumstances of the company in question. It could be anything from better access to overseas markets, lower taxes, lower labour costs, quicker delivery or a combination of any of these.

I But it would be fair to say the financial benefits are the main incentive, wouldn't it?

C In most cases it probably would, yes. Without them, I suppose few companies would be that interested. But there are risks involved as well, you know.

I And what are those risks?

C Well, the most common mistake companies make is they only see the savings and don't bother to think about the effect on other key criteria like quality and delivery. A clothing company that only buys from Asian suppliers at low cost, for instance, will find that as labour rates increase over time, it'll have to island hop to find new low cost sites. And this, of course, introduces uncertainty about quality—and that's critical for a clothing company. There are other possible risks as well.

I Such as?

C Well, such as negative publicity as a result of poor working conditions in the supplier's country. And, of course, there's always currency exchange risk.

I So how do you go about weighing up all these factors and choosing a supplier?

C It's crucial that companies know precisely what they're after from a supplier and that they fully understand their key selection criteria. They need to be careful to define them and make sure they're measurable and then rank them. It's dangerous selecting a particular supplier just because they happen to deliver outstanding performance in one objective such as cost or flexibility.

I So, having selected a prospective partner, what then?

C Well, then you have to negotiate how closely the two parties need to work together. If it's going to be a long-term relationship, you need to discuss how much sharing of information and resources will be necessary to extract maximum value from the collaboration. The prospective partners need to sit down and decide on the best form for the relationship to take.

I   And what's the most common form of this relationship?

C   Well, once again it depends on individual circumstances. The relationship can be anything, I suppose, from complete ownership through strategic alliances to buying the market.

I   Buying the market? What's that?

C   That's when companies just publish their specifications and ask prequalified vendors to bid for the contract. General Electric is currently doing $1bn of business this way over the Internet. It's a short-term deal with almost no interaction with the supplier and the length of the bidding process is cut by half. But most importantly for companies like GE, order processing is $5 an order as opposed to $50 when it's done on paper.

I   You mentioned strategic alliances. When do they make sense?

C   Well, for an aircraft manufacturer like Boeing, for example, an alliance with its engine manufacturers is logical because of the complex interaction between the body of the aircraft and its engines. And this complexity means everything has to be developed together. The arrangement also has the added bonus of reducing the financial risk of long-term development programmes.

I   And how about actually owning the supplier, then? When is that preferable?

C   Well, companies take over suppliers when they're vulnerable to fluctuations in the availability of key supplies. Take Du Pont, for example, the chemicals giant. Since oil is a primary ingredient of many of its products, Du Pont is very much affected by the availability, and therefore cost, of oil. Du Pont reduced these uncertainties by purchasing Conoco, its main oil supplier.

I   Thus keeping its costs down.

C   Possibly. Owning the supplier definitely increases financial control of the supply chain. But when you take the cost of acquisition into account, there are no short-term savings.

I   So, all in all, does global sourcing make sense?

C   Well, there are lots of very powerful benefits but managers have to consider all the main operational factors very carefully first.

Words and expressions

acquisition	/ˌækwɪˈzɪʃən/	*n.*	收购	maximum	/ˈmæksɪməm/ *adj.*	最大的；最高的
alliance	/əˈlaɪəns/	*n.*	联盟	precisely	/prɪˈsaɪslɪ/ *adv.*	准确地；确切地
catalyst	/ˈkætəlɪst/	*n.*	催化剂	vulnerable	/ˈvʌlnərəbl/ *adj.*	脆弱的；敏感的
collaboration	/kəˌlæbəˈreɪʃən/	*n.*	合作	bid for		投标
crucial	/ˈkruːʃəl/	*adj.*	决定性的；至	General Electric		通用电气集团
			关重要的	island hop		跳岛（在不同地方之间往来）
fluctuation	/ˌflʌktjʊˈeɪʃən/	*n.*	波动，起伏	look further afield		开阔视野
incentive	/ɪnˈsentɪv/	*n.*	动机；刺激	weigh up		衡量

Comprehension tasks

Read the text and answer the following questions.

1. What is the main attraction of global sourcing?
2. What is the most common mistake companies make when sourcing globally?
3. What is the most important decision once a partner is selected?
4. What is the main advantage of "buying the market"?

Read the text again and choose the correct answer to complete each sentence.

1. Global sourcing has become so widespread because of the increasing
   a. number of international mergers.
   b. competitiveness of foreign markets.
   c. efficiency of global communications.

2. When deciding on criteria for choosing a supplier, managers should
   a. insist on consistently outstanding performance.
   b. list and prioritise all their main objectives.
   c. be as flexible as possible with their criteria.

3. Strategic alliances make sense when
   a. components are mutually dependent.
   b. projects have a high level of financial risk.
   c. development programmes are long-term.

4. Ownership of the supplier is preferable when

    a. a company relies heavily on overseas suppliers.

    b. cost savings are the most important factor.

    c. access to vital resources is variable.

Vocabulary

Complete the sentences with the prepositions in the box.

~~of~~	with	up	into	in	to	for

1. By centralising production at our Slovakia plant, we've been able to realise substantial economies _of_ scale.

2. Because we localise our products, overseas customers are more able to identify ____ them.

3. We weighed ____ all the factors and decided to look for a joint venture partner.

4. I think the main catalyst ____ change was the creation of the single European currency.

5. Our first plant there was a big risk as we had little expertise ____ the region.

6. After problems with quality, we decided to shift ____ a long-term supplier relationship strategy and invested in equipment and training for our main supplier.

7. The aggressive growth strategy saw us expand ____ several new territories.

Match the adjectives with nouns by use of linking lines.

1. economic   a. presence
2. cultural   b. necessity
3. global   c. process
4. supply   d. criteria
5. key   e. stereotype
6. bidding   f. chain
7. tight   g. deadlines

Complete the following text with the words and phrases in the box.

while	therefore	however	similarly
means that	as opposed to	although	

Increased exposure to international business (1) _____ Japanese companies are not always as traditional as in the past. (2) _____, there are still a number of important cultural factors which need to be considered when doing business in Japan.

- During negotiations, it is common for there to be long periods of silence (3) _____ your Japanese colleagues formulate their response.
- The Japanese will still usually avoid saying "no". You may (4) _____ leave a meeting with the wrong impression.
- Japanese meetings tend to be more formal than those in the U.S.A., with people being addressed by their title and surname (5) _____ their first names.
- Dress is a very important issue for the Japanese, with a smart suit and tie the expected dress code in all business situations.
- Business remains still very much a male domain and (6) _____ inroads have been made by Japanese women, it is still unusual to find them in high level positions. (7) _____, workers in senior positions tend to be older than their counterparts in the U.S.A.

Listening

TASK 6 You will hear a sales executive presenting a computer system for electronic meetings. Identify the three major parts of this presentation.

Part 1: _____

Part 2: _____

Part 3: _____

TASK 7 Listen for details. Complete the notes using up to three words or a number. You will hear the recording TWICE.

Part 1

1. DecisionMaker® allows you to hold electronic meetings on _____.
2. Using computers enables people to express ideas freely without _____.

Part 2

3. The system generates more ideas by using the _____ of the entire group.
4. The system encourages _____ by keeping the proposer's identity secret.
5. Each idea is judged _____ rather than attitudes towards the proposer.
6. As a result of this team ownership of any proposals made, ideas are _____, allowing them to be processed more quickly.

7. Equal contributions mean _____ of the meeting by individuals.

8. Automatic documentation means a _____ is not required.

Part 3

9. The Whiteboard® means that _____ are accessible to the group.

10. FileShare® allows for the _____ within the group.

11. Consensus® offers three possible _____ for indicating opinions.

12. Briefcase® allows you to use your _____ in the meeting.

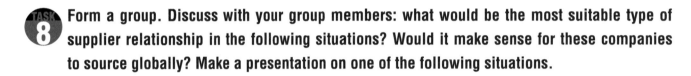

Business communication

Form a group. Discuss with your group members: what would be the most suitable type of supplier relationship in the following situations? Would it make sense for these companies to source globally? Make a presentation on one of the following situations.

- a car manufacturer sourcing a brake system
- a toy company sourcing a range of plastic dolls
- a restaurant sourcing its food supplies

Translation

Translate the following sentences into Chinese.

1. Hyper-competitive domestic markets have driven companies to look further afield in their search for competitive advantage. Although I think the process has really been accelerated by rapid advances in IT and telecoms.

   _____

   _____

2. A clothing company that only buys from Asian suppliers at low cost will find that as labour rates increase over time, it'll have to island hop to find new low cost sites.

   _____

   _____

3. It's a short-term deal with almost no interaction with the supplier and the length of the bidding process is cut by half. But most importantly for companies like GE, order processing is $5 an order as opposed to $50 when it's done on paper.

_____

_____

4. Popular approaches involve taking a more strategic approach and planning a new outsourcing initiative: increase the scope of service; transform the process rather than simply lifting and shifting; invest in more robust service integration and transition; use a third-party advisor.

_____

_____

5. Companies must become more sensitive and rigorous to understand the costs and risks involved in their decision. They also need to differentiate themselves through their global sourcing activities, either through cost, quality, brand or environmental approaches.

_____

_____

TASK
10

Translate the following sentences into English.

1. 许多公司表示应该改变自己的外包战略。他们正在考虑如何变更解决方案，如何建立一个能持续鼓励创新的激励机制，以及如何落实并管理这个新的外包战略。（incentive）

_____

_____

2. 在提升业绩表现方面表现突出的企业能够快速推进全球采购战略，大幅削减成本，并通过外包制造业务利用并扩大品牌价值。（performance）

_____

_____

3. 为全球采购团队提供可以用来跟踪工作进度并记录外包活动的工具十分重要。建立全球平台能帮助外包团队输入并查询业务活动，同时促进地域间的协同合作与沟通。（collaboration）

_____

_____

4. 企业建立战略联盟通常是为了涉足相关业务或开拓市场，特别是开拓政府为保护本土产业而限制进口地区的市场。（alliance）

_____

_____

5. IBM 认为，全球销售团队的推广能够大幅提升被收购公司的营业额，有时能够在收购完成后头一两年将营业额提升 40% 以上。（acquisition）

_____

_____

Writing

TASK 11 Suppose you work for QuayWest, a leisurewear retailer. Read the email, letter and notes below, which have been sent to you by colleagues and a customer. Write suitable replies. Remember the following.

- Who is the reader? What level of formality is appropriate?
- How long should each reply be?
- How should each reply be organised?
- What standard phrases will be useful?

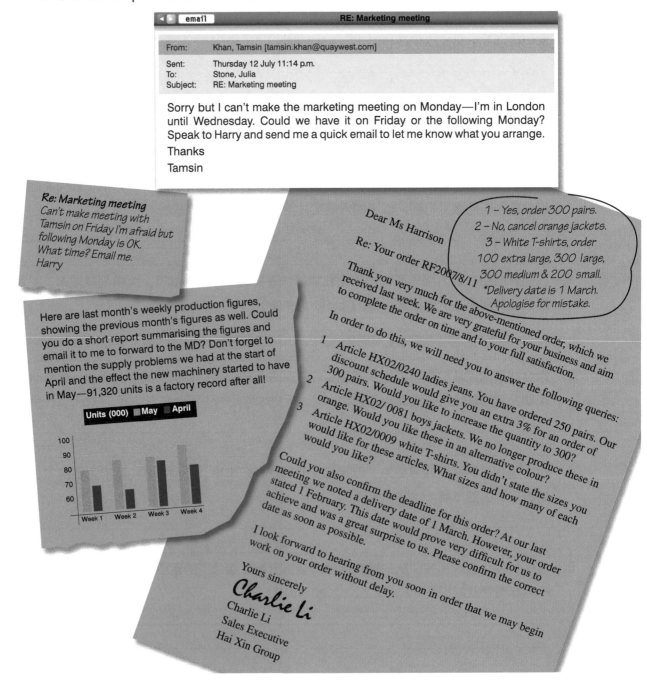

email

From:	Khan, Tamsin [tamsin.khan@quaywest.com]
Sent:	Thursday 12 July 11:14 p.m.
To:	Stone, Julia
Subject:	RE: Marketing meeting

RE: Marketing meeting

Sorry but I can't make the marketing meeting on Monday—I'm in London until Wednesday. Could we have it on Friday or the following Monday? Speak to Harry and send me a quick email to let me know what you arrange.

Thanks

Tamsin

Re: Marketing meeting
Can't make meeting with Tamsin on Friday I'm afraid but following Monday is OK. What time? Email me.
Harry

1 – Yes, order 300 pairs.
2 – No, cancel orange jackets.
3 – White T-shirts, order 100 extra large, 300 large, 300 medium & 200 small.
*Delivery date is 1 March. Apologise for mistake.

Here are last month's weekly production figures, showing the previous month's figures as well. Could you do a short report summarising the figures and email it to me to forward to the MD? Don't forget to mention the supply problems we had at the start of April and the effect the new machinery started to have in May—91,320 units is a factory record after all!

Units (000) ■ May ■ April

Week 1   Week 2   Week 3   Week 4

Dear Ms Harrison

Re: Your order RF2007/8/11

Thank you very much for the above-mentioned order, which we received last week. We are very grateful for your business and aim to complete the order on time and to your full satisfaction.

In order to do this, we will need you to answer the following queries:

1   Article HX02/0240 ladies jeans. You have ordered 250 pairs. Our discount schedule would give you an extra 3% for an order of 300 pairs. Would you like to increase the quantity to 300?
2   Article HX02/0081 boys jackets. We no longer produce these in orange. Would you like these in an alternative colour?
3   Article HX02/0009 white T-shirts. You didn't state the sizes you would like for these articles. What sizes and how many of each would you like?

Could you also confirm the deadline for this order? At our last meeting we noted a delivery date of 1 March. However, your order stated 1 February. This date would prove very difficult for us to achieve and was a great surprise to us. Please confirm the correct date as soon as possible.

I look forward to hearing from you soon in order that we may begin work on your order without delay.

Yours sincerely

Charlie Li

Charlie Li
Sales Executive
Hai Xin Group

Business know-how

Read the following passage and make an oral summary of the main points to your partner or group.

Crowdsourcing（众包）

Crowdsourcing is a sourcing model in which individuals or organisations obtain goods and services. These services include ideas and finances, from a large, relatively open and often rapidly-evolving group of Internet users; it divides work between participants to achieve a cumulative result. The word crowdsourcing itself is a portmanteau（手提箱）of crowd and outsourcing, and was coined in 2005. As a mode of sourcing, crowdsourcing existed prior to the digital age (i.e. "offline").

There are major differences between crowdsourcing and outsourcing. Crowdsourcing comes from a less-specific, more public group, whereas outsourcing is commissioned from a specific, named group, and includes a mix of bottom-up and top-down processes. Advantages of using crowdsourcing may include improved costs, speed, quality, flexibility, scalability（可扩缩性）, or diversity.

Some forms of crowdsourcing, such as in "idea competitions" or "innovation contests" provide ways for organisations to learn beyond the "base of minds" provided by their employees (e.g. LEGO Ideas). Tedious "microtasks" performed in parallel by large, paid crowds (e.g. Amazon Mechanical Turk) are another form of crowdsourcing. It has also been used by not-for-profit organisations and to create common goods (e.g. Wikipedia). The effect of user communication and the platform presentation should be taken into account when evaluating the performance of ideas in crowdsourcing contexts.

Text B Choosing a supplier

QuayWest, a European clothing company, has shortlisted five suppliers for its new range of leisurewear.

Consort Trading Co. Ltd.
Yungtong-Dong 968, Korea

By far the most reasonably priced of the potential suppliers, this medium-sized company exports to many countries in Asia, the Pacific Rim and Europe. The company is well-established and employs a large but poorly paid workforce. This, along with obvious lack of investment in new plant, probably explains how the company is able to produce at such exceptionally low costs. These factors, however, also account for the modest quality of the goods, some of which could even fail to meet European standards. It seems that the supplier would be in a position to deliver within satisfactory times and the owners insist that they would be flexible enough to deal with last-minute orders. However, a supplier relationship with this company could possibly have serious PR implications.

Samokovska, Inc.
Plodiv 4003, Bulgaria

This small but very modern company has been supplying EU countries for several years now. This experience shows in the level of workmanship and has resulted in the company adopting a policy of ensuring that each item within its catalogue conforms to all E.U. specifications. However, the variety of the catalogue is somewhat limited—as is the company's production capacity. It appears the company has decided on a strategy of offering an exclusive selection of high-quality, expensive products. It seems unlikely that the company would be versatile enough to respond quickly enough to market changes or deal with orders at short notice. Moreover, although the delivery times are quite impressive, the company would struggle to maintain these when faced with larger orders.

Namlong

The Namlong Sportswear Company Ltd.
Bangkok 10150, Thailand

One of the largest textile suppliers in Thailand, the Namlong Sportswear Company is a large enterptise with several factories in the Bangkok area. The company employs a large workforce and relies extensively on manual labour. However, the scale of its resources means it is very flexible and its production cycles are relatively short, even for large orders. These factors, along with impressive distribution, allow the company to respond to any changes in order specifications or schedules while meeting tight deadlines. There may be some room for negotiation on prices, which look relatively expensive compared to many of Namlong's competitors in the area, especially when the slightly disappointing standard of workmanship is taken into account.

Shiva

Shiva Trading Co. Ltd.
Mumbai 400034, India

The Shiva Trading Company is a small but well-established family-owned business that has been exporting throughout the sub-continent and is now looking to enter the European market. To help with this expansion, it is offering very reasonable prices to potential European customers, especially in relation to the satisfactory levels of quality that its products display. On the other hand, its present size and limited capacity could lead to delays and a certain amount of inflexibility in terms of schedules and short notice orders. However, the owners insist that planned expansion of the premises will ease these pressures by increasing capacity and reducing production cycles, thus enabling the company to turn orders around more efficiently.

Hai Xin Group Co. Ltd.
Shanghai 200051, China

This dynamic young company is looking for sales outlets in Europe. Although its goods tend to be slightly pricey, their quality is acceptable, with some evidence of attention to detail. However, it is not clear as yet whether these goods will conform to all E.U. regulations. The owners are confident, though, that their modern machinery and flexible production processes mean that the company will be able to cope with any changes in product specifications and garment features necessary to meet legal requirements. This flexibility also means that the company has already built up an impressively varied catalogue, with many items offering optional and additional features. This would suggest that introducing new product lines would not be a problem. Hai Xin also appears able to offer satisfactory delivery times.

Words and expressions

exceptionally /ɪkˈsepʃənəlɪ/	*adv.* 罕见地；异常地	workforce /ˈwɜːkfɔːs/	*n.* 劳动力
garment /ˈɡɑːmənt/	*n.* 衣服；外观	workmanship /ˈwɜːkmənʃɪp/	*n.* 工艺
implication /ˌɪmplɪˈkeɪʃən/	*n.* 可能引发的后果	conform to	与……一致
lack /læk/	*n.* 缺乏，不足	PR (Public Relation)	公共关系
plant /plɑːnt/	*n.* 工厂；车间	production cycle	生产周期
pricey /ˈpraɪsɪ/	*adj.* 价格高的	short notice	临时通知
versatile /ˈvɜːsətaɪl/	*adj.* 万能的	the Pacific Rim	环太平洋地区
well-established /ˈwelɪˈstæblɪʃt/	*adj.* 已树立声誉的		

Comprehension tasks

Match each of the following statements with a company mentioned in the text.

1. This supplier is able to offer a wide range of products.
2. There is a lot of old machinery in this supplier's factory.
3. This supplier is able to manufacture to the highest standards.
4. Orders are delivered extremely quickly by this supplier.
5. This supplier is hoping to improve its delivery times in the near future.
6. Doing business with this supplier could harm the company's reputation.
7. This supplier would be unable to adapt its product lines quickly.
8. This is the best supplier in terms of the relationship between price and quality.

Read the text again and answer the following questions.

1. What are the reasons for the exceptionally low costs of production in Consorting Trading?
2. What is the strategy that Samokovska has decided for its limited variety of catalogue?
3. Why is there some room for negotiation on prices with The Namlong Sportswear?
4. According to the owners of The Shiva Trading Company, will the present size and limited capacity lead to delays and inflexibility? Why or why not?
5. What seems to be the weakness of Hai Xin Group?

Vocabulary

Match the words with their synonyms by use of linking lines.

1. specification   buildings
2. warranty   measurement
3. attraction   machinery
4. reputation   guarantee
5. plant   incentive
6. premises   image

Complete the word diagram with the phrases in the box.

~~increased profits~~	negative publicity	strategic alliance	lower labour costs
lower quality	buying the market	competitive advantage	
shorter time to market	cultural differences	currency exchange fluctuations	
global presence	access to markets	full ownership	

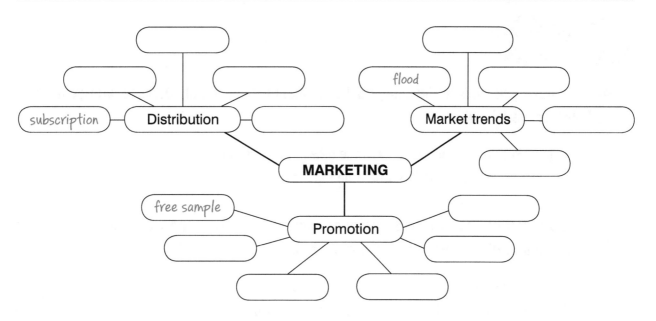

 Choose the correct word to fill each gap.

"Buying the market" is an arrangement whereby companies publish component (1) _____ and ask pre-qualified vendors to bid for the contract. It is a short-term deal with almost no (2) _____ with the supplier and the length of the bidding process is (3) _____ by half. Furthermore, the cost of order (4) _____ falls to around $5 an order as (5) _____ to $50 when it is done on paper. For companies such as aircraft manufacturer Boeing, (6) _____, such an arrangement with its engine suppliers would be unsuitable because of the complex (7) _____ between the body of the aircraft and its engines. For companies like Boeing, strategic (8) _____ make far more sense because they allow the company to work (9) _____ with its supplier, developing the aircraft's engines together. An added (10) _____ of this collaboration is that it reduces the financial risks of development programmes.

1.   a. standards   b. specifications   c. criteria
2.   a. exchange   b. feedback   c. communication
3.   a. decreased   b. reduced   c. limited
4.   a. processing   b. developing   c. delivering
5.   a. contrary   b. opposed   c. different

6. a. although   b. nevertheless   c. however
7. a. structure   b. interaction   c. collaboration
8. a. relationships   b. alliances   c. arrangements
9. a. closely   b. precisely   c. mutually
10. a. potential   b. satisfaction   c. benefit

Speaking

TASK 6 Suppose you work in the QuayWest Purchasing Department. Discuss with your partner and decide the following.

- your key criteria for suppliers of the new range of leisurewear
- which of the five suppliers would be the most suitable

TASK 7 Would you use each of the following suppliers? Form a pair and discuss the following situations with your partner. State your reasons.

1. Using this supplier is unlikely to enhance our image.
2. It's uncertain whether they'll conform to standards.
3. Recent changes have lengthened production cycles.
4. The company has a comprehensive catalogue.
5. Their standard of workmanship is encouraging.
6. Exchange rates would be a factor with this supplier.
7. They fulfil our key selection criteria.
8. Short notice orders might cause potential complications.

Business communication

TASK 8 Visit the Nestle website https://www.nestle.com/. Find out information about Nestle's sourcing standards. What else should a company consider besides price, quality, delivery and flexibility when choosing suppliers? Discuss with your partner and make a one-minute presentation. The following principles may give you some hints.

The Big 5 Executive Summary Principles

1. Nestle staff sources with care and respect for the people, planet and oceans where materials and services are produced.

2. Tier 1 Suppliers apply good labour standards in recruiting, compensating, and caring about their workforce. Preserving natural resources and conducting business in an ethical and collaborative way is ensured.

3. Intermediaries operate with the same principles of value, transparency and respect as their suppliers and clients, nurturing traceability and preserving information.

4. Origins, farmers and fishers, continuously improve their ways of working in:
   • Optimising yield through conservative agriculture, preservation of soil biome and rationalisation of agrochemical inputs,
   • Caring and respecting the workforce, animals, land, water and forests that they work with.

5. Supply Chain Tiers work in compliance with applicable regulations, continuously monitor, disclose, and improve against the Standard.

Translation

 Translate the following sentences into Chinese.

1. It seems that the supplier would be in a position to deliver within satisfactory times and the owners insist that they would be flexible enough to deal with last-minute orders.

   _____

   _____

2. This experience shows in the level of workmanship and has resulted in the company adopting a policy of ensuring that each item within its catalogue conforms to all E.U. specifications.

   _____

   _____

3. On the other hand, its present size and limited capacity could lead to delays and a certain amount of inflexibility in terms of schedules and short notice orders.

   _____

   _____

4. Decades of outsourcing of American jobs overseas has drastically altered both the country's economy and the lives of millions. Cheaper labour in developing nations meant that many jobs, like telecommunications and factory work, were sent abroad.

_____

_____

5. Corporations' globalised marketing and sourcing strategies influence people's lifestyle choices and define the socioeconomic environment within which they make these choices.

_____

_____

TASK 10 **Translate the following sentences into English.**

1. 全球采购占据了大部分行业多于 50% 的制造总成本。因此，采购组织扮演着比以往更重要的战略性角色，它们通过维持低成本以及有效并高效地提供产品服务，帮助公司获得并维持竞争优势。(account for)

_____

_____

2. 一些公共领域的采购者正在结束供应商所谓"先搞定再搞大"的策略，运用这一策略的公司一开始出价很低，取得合约后便通过增加工作量或者争论合同细节来抬升价格。(specification)

_____

_____

3. 中国生产商正转移现有部分资金投资海外工厂，以便在快速发展的市场进行生产和销售，而不受关税的影响。(capacity)

_____

_____

4. 不是所有地区的销售商都会从供应链的角度思考，不过他们确实应该如此。面临不断增长的成本、高标准的顾客和极薄的利润，供应链管理往往可以让经销公司从同行中脱颖而出。(distribution)

_____

_____

5. 无论是大型还是知名的公司，都无法抵御全球灾难。然而在出现问题时，一家企业如何应对则会意味着完全不同的结果，可能是一场迅速的变革，也可能让问题变得更严重。(well-established)

_____

_____

Write a report recommending the most suitable supplier of the five suppliers in Text B for QuayWest and giving reasons for your decision.

Warming up

 What makes an ethical company? What responsibilities should a company undertake?

 Which of the following statements about ethics do you agree with?

- Ethics provide the rules within which an organisation must conduct itself.
- Ethics show an organisation's attitude towards society.
- Ethics are a source of competitive advantage.

Text A　Ethical practice report

The following is the extract from the Deerwode Ethical Practice report.

Ethical practice in the workplace

Summary of findings

In April 2010, a questionnaire was sent to the CEOs and senior managers of 500 U.K. companies, which had been selected on the basis of size in terms of number of employees. In response to an increasing level of interest expressed by managers in the public sector led us to extend our sample to include the senior executives of a further 20 organisations in the public sector, most of whom were involved in working with the health sector in some way.

Key findings

According to the survey, when executives described an organisation as "highly ethical", the factors considered most important were fair employment practices, legal compliance and the delivery of high-quality goods and services. Corporate philanthropy was given the least weight in making this judgement.

It was found that 38% of the organisations surveyed had formal policies to protect employees who report ethical or legal violations, i.e. whistle blowers, an increase of 22% reported in the previous survey. In total, written statements of values and principles were produced by 85% of participating organisations.

Deerwode devised a list of issues relating to company integrity against which managers had to indicate the level of attention each issue received in their organisation. The results can be seen below. Of these issues, the two most frequently identified as of greatest concern for the next three to five years were security of information and environmental issues. Security of information was also the issue with which respondents were least satisfied with current efforts.

London, May 2011

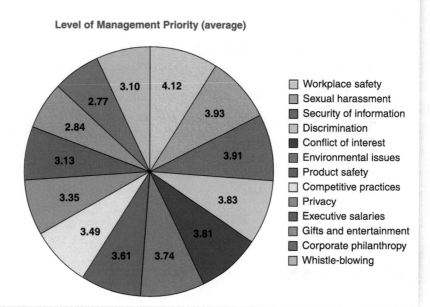

Level of Management Priority (average)

- Workplace safety
- Sexual harassment
- Security of information
- Discrimination
- Conflict of interest
- Environmental issues
- Product safety
- Competitive practices
- Privacy
- Executive salaries
- Gifts and entertainment
- Corporate philanthropy
- Whistle-blowing

Words and expressions

compliance /kəm'plaɪəns/	*n.* 遵守	**respondent** /rɪ'spɒndənt/	*n.* 调查对象,（调查表的）答卷人
devise /dɪ'vaɪz/	*v.* 设计		
harassment /'hærəsmənt/	*n.* 骚扰	**give weight (to)**	给……以分量；重视
integrity /ɪn'tegrɪtɪ/	*n.* 正直	**in response to**	以回应……
philanthropy /fɪ'lænθrəpɪ/	*n.* 慈善	**whistle blower**	告发者，告密者

Comprehension tasks

Read the text and circle "True" or "False". Correct the false statements.

1. The questionnaire was sent to a total of 500 senior executives.　　True/False
2. It was thought to be of great importance to support good causes.　　True/False
3. Fewer than half of the participating companies protect whistle blowers.　　True/False
4. Most CEOs were content with existing information security measures.　　True/False

Read the text again. Supply the details concerning important ethical factors according to the extract.

1. Fair employment practices: _____
2. Legal compliance: _____
3. The delivery of high-quality goods and services: _____
4. Written statements of values and principles: _____
5. Security of information: _____
6. Environmental issues: _____

Vocabulary

Which word does not go with the word in the capital letters in each group?

1. ETHICAL
   gossip　　dilemma　　behaviour　　investment
2. OFFICIAL
   warning　　policy　　prejudice　　guidelines
3. CORPORATE
   philanthropy　　privacy　　gift-giving　　guidelines
4. LEGAL
   harassment　　action　　proceedings　　compliance
5. SECURITY
   password　　measures　　procedures　　perpetrator
6. ETHNIC
   minority　　diversity　　mismanagement　　origin

Put ethical issues in the box on the line of each situation.

~~information security~~	racial discrimination	executive salaries	conflict of interest
environmental issues	workplace safety	product safety	whistle-blowing
competitive practices	sexual harassment	legal compliance	privacy
gifts and entertainment/corporate gift-giving		delivery of high quality goods and services	
corporate philanthropy		fair employment practices	
industrial espionage（商业间谍）		financial mismanagement	

1. employees copying confidential data onto disks
   information security

2. physically intimidating the opposite sex

3. accidents occurring at work

4. conforming to government legislation

5. senior managers receiving massive pay increases

6. rewarding clients with expensive freebies

7. not treating people from ethnic minorities equally

8. reporting breaches of a company's ethical code

Match the words and then use them to complete the sentences below.

foul	blower
information	play
good	sector
industrial	correctness
political	practices
shady	causes
public	security
whistle	espionage

1. The company suspected _foul play_ so it hired a security expert to find out whether someone was giving confidential information to a competitor.

2. In the present atmosphere of _____, you have to be very careful what you say to colleagues at work. An inappropriate joke could be seen as harassment.

3. It takes a lot of courage to be a(an) _____. Powerful companies can put a lot of pressure on employees not to go to the press with stories of corporate wrong-doing.

4. The company donates a lot of money to _____. It also encourages staff to support charities by matching any private donations they give.

5. Hacking into another company's computers is a very rare form of _____. Computer hackers are normally individuals who target a company.

6. We're tightening up our _____ by issuing log-on passwords to all staff.

7. If they can't compete fairly, some companies resort to _____.

8. As there is no competition or profit-making in the _____, there are very few cases of industrial espionage.

Listening

TASK 6 Rick Haywood, Managing Director of electronics wholesaler Octacon, discusses information security with two colleagues. Listen and identify the problem.

TASK 7 Listen to the rest of the discussion and complete the table.

Action discussed	Implications

Business communication

 Suppose you work in a multinational company. For more social engagement and business opportunities, the multinational company you work for is considering helping the local small enterprises in your city with their business growth. You have been asked to give some recommendations. Discuss the situation with your partner and decide:

- considering business ethics, what kind of local enterprises you should choose;
- in what way you may offer help.

Translation

Translate the following sentences into Chinese.

1. In response to an increasing level of interest expressed by managers in the public sector led us to extend our sample to include the senior executives of a further 20 organisations in the public sector, most of whom were involved in working with the health sector in some way.

2. When executives described an organisation as "highly ethical", the factors considered most important were fair employment practices, legal compliance and the delivery of high-quality goods and services.

3. Of these issues, the two most frequently identified as of greatest concern for the next three to five years were security of information and environmental issues. Security of information was also the issue with which respondents were least satisfied with current efforts.

4. More and more companies are realising how ethics can be an important competitive advantage in the global economy. Companies that are ethical tend to realise that doing the right thing is actually good for business—and they drive and encourage a culture that emphasises that.

5. Networking can be useful not only for identifying job openings, but also in assessing how specific organisations may interpret ethics—for instance, if they view it as synonymous with compliance or instead see the issue as having broader strategic implications.

_____

_____

TASK 10 **Translate the following sentences into English.**

1. 私营和公共领域的受访者都认为，在工作中撒谎是新兴市场里的一个普遍问题。然而在供应链关系中，造成更加严重后果的违规更为常见，比如行贿和隐藏不当行为。(sector)

_____

_____

2. 在当今社交媒体驱动的文化下，道德上踏错一步就可能毁掉一个企业。另一方面，遵守规定和道德可以让企业区别于其他竞争者。因为企业需要保证与之合作的第三方不会给他们带来麻烦。(compliance)

_____

_____

3. 相当一部分的消费者在做购买决策时认为一个品牌的道德很重要，且更有可能考虑和推荐一个哪怕只做了一点慈善的品牌。并且，消费者相信企业有责任确保有道德的供应链。(give weight to)

_____

_____

4. 每个企业都必须设立道德准则，如诚信、透明、勤奋等，清晰定义企业可接受的和不可接受的行为，这有助于员工以此为导向来检查自身的行为。(code)

_____

_____

5. 如今，品牌为了达到领先，必须不能满足于简单证明他们的产品略胜一筹，想要树立品牌形象的聪明企业还需要努力展示他们的价值观。(values)

_____

_____

Writing

TASK 11 **Use the Internet to find out about a company that has been accused of ethical misconduct. Write a report on the case, suggesting what could have been done to prevent it and what measures could still be put in place.**

Business know-how

Read the following passage and make an oral summary of the main points to your partner or group.

Corporate social responsibility (企业社会责任)

Corporate social responsibility (CSR) is a self-regulating business model that helps a company be socially accountable—to itself, its stakeholders, and the public. By practicing corporate social responsibility, also called corporate citizenship, companies can be conscious of the kind of impact they are having on all aspects of society including economic, social, and environmental. To engage in CSR means that, in the normal course of business, a company is operating in ways that enhance society and the environment, instead of contributing negatively to it.

Corporate social responsibility is a broad concept that can take many forms depending on the company and industry. Through CSR programmes, philanthropy, and volunteer efforts, businesses can benefit society while boosting their own brands. As important as CSR is for the community, it is equally valuable for a company. CSR activities can help forge a stronger bond between employee and corporation; they can boost morale and can help both employees and employers feel more connected with the world around them.

In order for a company to be socially responsible, it first needs to be responsible to itself and its shareholders. Often, companies that adopt CSR programmes have grown their business to the point where they can give back to society. Thus, CSR is primarily a strategy of large corporations. Also, the more visible and successful a corporation is, the more responsibility it has to set standards of ethical behaviour for its peers, competition, and industry.

In 2010, the International Organisation for Standardisation (ISO, 国际标准化组织) released a set of voluntary standards meant to help companies implement corporate social responsibility. Unlike other ISO standards, ISO 26000 provides guidance rather than requirements because the nature of CSR is more qualitative than quantitative, and its standards cannot be certified. Instead, ISO 26000 clarifies what social responsibility is and helps organisations translate CSR principles into effective actions. The standard is aimed at all types of organisations regardless of their activity, size, or location. And, because many key stakeholders from around the world contributed to developing ISO 26000, this standard represents an international consensus (共识).

Text B   Ethical issues

Five people talk about unethical behaviour at their companies.

Speaker 1   I suppose, in a way, it's a kind of generation thing. When George started, there was no such thing as political correctness in the office environment. In those days, I'm sure it was common practice to call colleagues "love" or "darling", pay compliments about their figures or even give them gifts and things. But you just can't do that nowadays and he should have known better. He says his secretary never complained about it to him in person and that if she had, he'd have stopped doing it, but she didn't. Instead, she went straight to the board and warned them that she'd take legal action if nothing was done about it. Well, they soon hauled George in and explained the situation. George was outraged and told them what they could do with the job there and then.

Speaker 2   If you'd looked around the workplace, I guess you would have seen the evidence. I mean, in a company of this size you would have expected to see at least some ethnic diversity in the workplace, wouldn't you? Anyway, someone finally discovered a secret file with all the applicants who were not given an interview. Whoever it was blew the whistle to the local press and that was it—the company was faced with a PR disaster and a police investigation. Of course, the first thing the board did was give the well-paid HR executive his marching orders and insist that it was his prejudice and not company policy. But if that was the case, then why hadn't they noticed what was going on?

Speaker 3   I'm sure Sharleen didn't think she was doing anything wrong at the time. She'd been told to put together a report on the market penetration of a new safety product we'd just launched. So she had to find out how much business our main rival was doing. OK, so hacking into their corporate intranet wasn't the right way of going about it—but no-one realised she was a complete whizzkid. Luckily, they didn't find out what happened. If they had, it would have cost us a fortune. You can imagine everyone's reaction when she announced what she'd done. Our Ethics Officer went mad and had to quickly put together an official code for dealing with competitors. As for Sharleen, well, she just got away without even so much as an official warning!

Speaker 4   We'd been doing business with them for years and our sales executives had always enjoyed very good relationships with them. I don't think for one minute it would have made any difference if we hadn't offered them the occasional thank you for their business. But we always thought of it as good customer relationship management. What's wrong with the odd weekend away for a loyal customer? Anyway, the new CEO changed all that. Maybe it was a cultural thing, I don't know, but she suspended all freebies pending a review. She also recruited someone to regulate dealings with our clients—a sort of moral policeman, I guess. She even wrote to all our customers warning them not to accept any kind of presents from any of our reps.

Speaker 5 Every business wants to be ethically sound but it's a hyper-competitive world out there and when you're under pressure to make money and keep to a budget, it's a different matter. Pete, the Production Manager, didn't like the new regulation spray paint—it just wasn't as good—so he carried on using the old stuff. He knew there'd be trouble if anyone found out. But I guess he just hoped they wouldn't. Of course, some campaigners tested the local water and found evidence of the banned chemicals. I suppose when you think about the PR nightmare that followed and the hefty fine the company had to pay, Pete was lucky to get away with just a letter threatening dismissal if he used the old paint ever again.

Words and expressions

board	/bɔːd/	*n.*	董事会	pending /'pendɪŋ/	*prep.*	直到……为止
campaigner	/kæm'peɪnə(r)/	*n.*	（争取变革的）活动家	rep /rep/ (representative)	*n.*	代表
code	/kəʊd/	*n.*	法规，规则	rival /'raɪvəl/	*n.*	竞争对手
freebie	/'friːbɪ/	*n.*	免费物	suspend /sə'spend/	*v.*	暂停；中止
hack	/hæk/	*v.*	非法入侵（计算机系统）	whizzkid /'wɪzkɪd/	*n.*	神童；奇才
haul	/hɔːl/	*v.*	（用力）拉，拖	in person		亲自；当面
hefty	/'heftɪ/	*adj.*	巨大的	market penetration		市场渗透
intranet	/'ɪntrənet/	*n.*	企业内部网；内联网	political correctness		政治正确
outrage	/'aʊtreɪdʒ/	*v.*	激怒			

Comprehension tasks

Read the text and decide which ethical issue and which consequence each speaker refers to.

Ethical issues

Which ethical issue does each speaker refer to?

1. _____
2. _____
3. _____
4. _____
5. _____

a. industrial espionage
b. workplace safety
c. racial discrimination
d. environmental protection
e. executive salaries
f. sexual harassment
g. financial mismanage
h. corporate gift-giving

Consequences

Which consequence does each speaker refer to?

1. _____
2. _____
3. _____
4. _____
5. _____

i. a manager was dismissed

j. computer security was reviewed

k. an ethics officer was appointed

l. the company informed the police

m. a written warning was given

n. the company produced guidelines

o. a consultant was brought in

p. the employee resigned

 Read the text again and circle "True" or "False". Correct the false statements.

1. George actually knows what he should not do, but he does what he thinks to be better. — True/False

2. It is not justified that a big company refuses to give an interview to applicants for ethnic reasons. — True/False

3. In order to spy on the business of their main rival, Sharleen has someone hack into the Internet system of the company. — True/False

4. The good relationships between the sales executives and their customers were built on freebies, according to the fourth speaker. — True/False

5. In the business world filled with fierce competition, it is not quite easy for a company to always practise ethical standards especially when there is a financial issue. — True/False

Vocabulary

 Match the words with their synonyms by use of linking lines.

1. survey   precaution
2. measure   questionnaire
3. conduct   gift
4. rule   competitor
5. threat   regulation
6. rival   behaviour
7. freebie   warning

TASK 4 **Match verbs with nouns and then use them to complete the sentences below.**

produce	the law
take	an imitation
hack into	a grudge
issue	a system
bear	a fine
commit	legal action
comply with	passwords
pay	a crime

1. One of our competitors managed to _produce an imitation_ of our secret recipe, which tasted exactly the same. That's when we suspected foul play.

2. Computer experts can _____ no matter how good its security is.

3. We're now under a lot of pressure to _____ on protecting whistle blowers.

4. Most people think they don't _____ when they take stationery home from work for private use but in reality it's a form of theft.

5. We used to _____ but too many people forgot them and had to ring the IT department saying they were locked out of the computer system.

6. We knew someone was deleting important data from the server, so we asked all the managers if they had any employees that might _____ against the company.

7. When their main rival brought out a similar product, they decided to _____ on the grounds of an infringement of their patent.

8. The company had to _____ after being found guilty of paying for information from employees of one of their rivals.

TASK 5 **Fill each gap with a suitable word.**

As you know, our company had been doing business out there for years, working with the smaller family-run firms. Nigel Beynon, (1) _____ was the Head of Purchasing for over fifteen years, had managed (2) _____ build up several solid relationships with local suppliers. In fact, I sometimes thought he felt (3) _____ at home out there than he (4) _____ back here in the U.K. Anyway, problems first arose (5) _____ one of the newspapers decided to do a feature (6) _____ ethics in the clothing industry. They discovered (7) _____ one of our suppliers was using child labour. It was (8) _____ much of a shock to Nigel as it was to everyone (9) _____. You see, he'd never actually visited (10) _____ single factory. He'd just believed the suppliers (11) _____ they assured him they conformed to our workplace standards. If only he (12) _____ taken the time to check their claims, he'd never have had to hand in his notice.

Speaking

6 According to ethical issues mentioned in the text, which ones should be most concerned in a company? Discuss with your partner.

7 Talk about one of the following topics with your partner.

- how to encourage ethical behaviour from employees
- the importance of ethics in today's business world

Business communication

8 Discuss with your partner and put the five cases of unethical behaviour mentioned in the text into order of seriousness. State your reasons.

Translation

9 Translate the following sentences into Chinese.

1. Whoever it was blew the whistle to the local press and that was it—the company was faced with a PR disaster and a police investigation. Of course, the first thing the board did was give the well-paid HR executive his marching orders and insist that it was his prejudice and not company policy.

2. Our Ethics Officer went mad and had to quickly put together an official code for dealing with competitors. As for Sharleen, she just got away without even so much as an official warning!

3. She suspended all freebies pending a review. She also recruited someone to regulate dealings with our clients—a sort of moral policeman. She even wrote to all our customers warning them not to accept any kind of presents from any of our reps.

4. Forty-seven percent of financial services professionals say it's likely that their competitors have committed unethical or illegal acts to gain an advantage in the market. Within their own companies, 23 percent believed their colleagues had acted that way.

_____

_____

5. Deliberate deception in the workplace includes taking credit for work done by someone else, calling in sick in order to go to the beach, sabotaging (妨碍) the work of another person and, in sales, misrepresenting the product or service to get the sale.

_____

_____

TASK 10 **Translate the following sentences into English.**

1. 许多人相信网络袭击的受害者不应该"反向入侵",主要是因为担心反向入侵可能是非法或不道德的。另外如果目标是外国网络,那么这一行为可能引发国家之间的网络战。(hack)

_____

_____

2. Facebook 可能被一家欧盟隐私监察组织罚款,数额高达 16.3 亿美元,原因是 Facebook 泄露了多达 5 000 万用户的个人信息。这次数据入侵可能违反了欧盟新隐私法,如果欧盟公民受到影响,则会导致巨额的罚款。(hefty)

_____

_____

3. 市场渗透战略中最有建设性的内容之一就是分销渠道。例如,如果你的公司最重要的收入来源是零售商店,那么可以尝试扩展其他渠道,比如利用区域代理等。(market penetration)

_____

_____

4. 如果你身带残疾,你的雇主就有法律义务处理这一问题。他们必须就你工作的方式或工作的地点做出"合理调整",因为以残疾为由的开除可能构成非法歧视。(dismissal)

_____

_____

5. 商业秘密是商业间谍活动最常见的目标之一。这样的信息能帮助商业对手提高其产品竞争力,或者比你更快地向市场推出类似产品。(industrial espionage)

_____

_____

Writing

TASK 11 Suppose your company has received a number of complaints from staff about their working conditions. The Human Resources Manager has asked you to write a report about the current situation. Write the report, including the reasons for the complaints and recommendations for dealing with them.

Warming up

TASK 1 Which of these can give you information about the performance of a company? The share price, the annual report, newspapers or magazines? Which information is the easiest to find? Which information do you think is the most accurate?

TASK 2 The words in the box are used to describe trends about the performance of a company. Choose the right word in the box for each trend.

to rise	to collapse	to recover	to shoot up	to peak	to fall

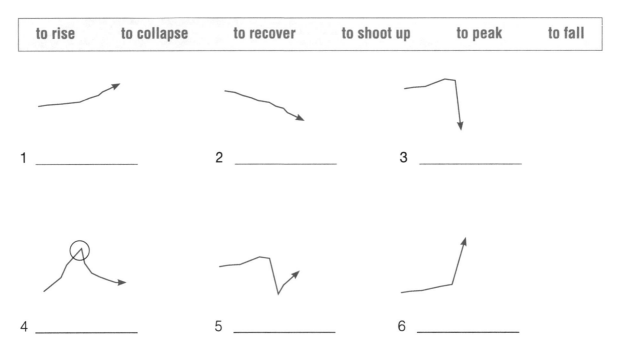

1 _____   2 _____   3 _____

4 _____   5 _____   6 _____

Text A A television report

The following is a television report about Fairways, a supermarket chain.

Tory: So, let's have a look at how the markets are doing with Jenny.

Jenny: Thanks, Tony. Well, we'll begin with Fairways, the supermarket chain. They've reported their results today. For the past six months, pre-tax profits rose sharply by 9.8%, which brought the final figure for the year to just over 6.3m. That's up from just over 5.8m last year. The dividend is up. If you're one of their shareholders, you can expect half a penny per share. Fairways has got 163 stores and three now actually sell petrol, so they do seem to be expanding. They've also just spent half a million pounds on buying e-shop services, which specialises in developing Internet-based home shopping. However, the business is only operating at break-even and isn't expected to do much more this year, it has to be said.

Now, let's take a look, shall we, at how Fairways' share price has done over the last 12 months. As you can see, it's been pretty volatile. After steady progress throughout the first half of the year, it really shot up at the end of the summer, when everyone thought there'd be a takeover. At the height of the rumours, in September, you can see that shares peaked at just over 80 pence. The takeover didn't happen, though, and the price collapsed. By mid-October it had fallen as far as the 55 pence mark. The shares recovered slowly to 65 pence by November, but then they went into steady decline again for the next two months, down once again to the 55 pence mark. However, news of good trading results has meant that shares have improved again this year. And it has to be said, the share price is marginally up on last February, so shareholders are in profit over the 12 month period. And if we look at the Fairways shares today, they're up slightly by 1.3 pence at 67 and a half.

Words and expressions

break-even /ˌbreɪkˈiːvən/	*n.*	盈亏平衡点	
collapse /kəˈlæps/	*v.*	暴跌	
dividend /ˈdɪvɪdend/	*n.*	红利；股息，股利	
marginally /ˈmɑːdʒɪnəlɪ/	*adv.*	微小地；少量地	
peak /piːk/	*v.*	达到高峰	
shareholder /ˈʃeəhəʊldə(r)/	*n.*	股东	

slightly /ˈslaɪtlɪ/	*adv.*	轻微地
steady /ˈstedɪ/	*adj.*	稳定的
takeover /ˈteɪkəʊvə(r)/	*n.*	收购
volatile /ˈvɒlətaɪl/	*adj.*	不稳定的，易波动的
pre-tax profit		税前利润
specialise in		专注于

Comprehension tasks

Read the text and answer the following questions.

1. What is Fairways' current strategy? Give examples.
2. How successful is the e-shop service?
3. Why did Fairways' share price rise so quickly?
4. What helped the share price at the start of 2011?

Read the text again and complete the graph below.

February 2010–February 2011

Vocabulary

TASK 3 Complete the description of the graph with the correct form of the verbs in the box.

recover	peak	fall	shoot up	collapse	rise

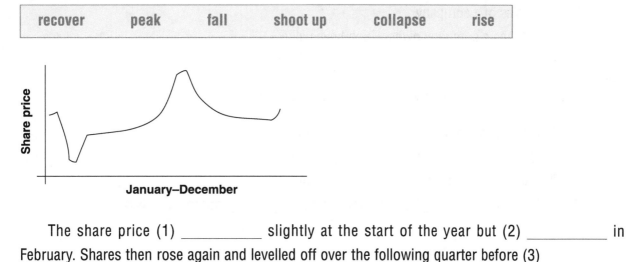

The share price (1) _____ slightly at the start of the year but (2) _____ in February. Shares then rose again and levelled off over the following quarter before (3) _____ in the summer. In August they finally (4) _____ and then started to (5) _____ steadily, dropping back to their spring level by the end of November. Rumours of good trading results led to a slight (6) _____ in the last few weeks, which returned shares to the same level as at the start of the year.

TASK 4 Complete the crossword.

Across

1. An annual payment made to shareholders
4. Before tax is deducted
5. A company's... activities are its most important

7. The purchase of another company

8. Money spent now in order to bring future benefit

Down

1. The sale of a subsidiary

2. … profit = profit after costs have been deducted

3. The sales of a company

6. The things a company owns which have value

 Complete each sentence with a suitable preposition.

1. The shares peaked _____ 260p in September.

2. Sales fell _____ £5.6m _____ £4.8m.

3. There was a decrease _____ net profit.

4. Sales rose _____ £2m. This was a rise _____ approximately 4%.

Listening

 The graph shows the price for Tesco shares over a three-month period. Fill in the blanks using the information you heard from the audio.

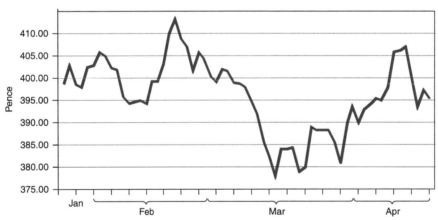

Richard: Now earlier you talked about Tesco, the U.K.'s largest supermarket chain. And I understand you have a (1) _____ illustrating what's been happening to their share price over the last three months.

Katie: Yes, and here it is. Now this is more or less (2) _____ of what's been happening throughout the sector for the last year, although Tesco being Tesco have been in a position to make themselves more (3) _____ to investors than perhaps any of their competitors. The price had been reasonably (4) _____ at the end of last year. But as you can see, in the period immediately after Christmas there were some (5) _____. The price finally recovered, even reaching a high towards the end of February. But then the price fell and fell, even despite some small rises, due mainly to (6) _____ from investors, I think. So that, by the middle of March the price had fallen to a low of 378, from a high of 413 three weeks previously. It then finally (7) _____, getting back to just over the 405 mark in April. It fell slightly, before settling back to around the 395 that it is today.

Richard: That's not another dip in consumer confidence bringing the price down from 413, is it?

Katie: No, I don't think so. We can expect a (8) _____ in spending in the months after Christmas, when not many of us have much spare cash to spend anyway. A fall in sales is fairly predictable at that time of year, and there's no suggestion of a price (9) _____. No, I think the reason is that those people who bought Tesco shares when they were round about 380 decided to take their profits and sell them once the price had reached £4.05 or (10) _____. If you had bought say 10,000 shares at 3.80 pounds and sold them at 4.05 pounds, you would have made a tidy £2,500. Not bad for a month's investment.

7 **Listen to the recording again and find examples of the following diagram.**

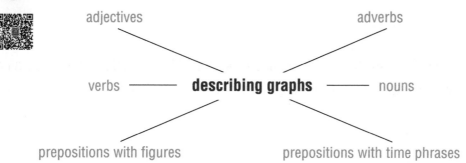

Business communication

8 **Work in pairs. Discuss the following topic with your partner.**

How common is investing in shares in your country?

Translation

Translate the following sentences into Chinese.

1. For the past six months, pre-tax profits rose sharply by 9.8%, which brought the final figure for the year to just over 6.3m. That's up from just over 5.8m last year. The dividend is up.

_____

2. They've also just spent half a million pounds on buying e-shop services, which specialises in developing Internet-based home shopping. However, the business is only operating at break-even and isn't expected to do much more this year, it has to be said.

_____

3. However, news of good trading results has meant that shares have improved again this year. And it has to be said, the share price is marginally up on last February, so shareholders are in profit over the 12 month period.

_____

4. The company will announce a "substantial" operating profit for 2013 later this month, according to Mr. Samuelson, as close to $250m of savings help the carmaker improve on a break-even position in 2012.

_____

5. The shares recovered slowly to 30 pence by June, but then they went into steady decline again for the next quarter, down once again to the 20 pence mark.

_____

Translate the following sentences into English.

1. 从 20 世纪 70 年代初开始，由于政治、经济等多方因素的影响，国际石油市场就一直很不稳定。（volatile）

_____

2. 该公司发言人拒绝向新闻界透露公司收购的详细情况，因为他们认为过早披露信息会影响公司的股票价格。（takeover）

_____

_____

3. 虽然大幅削减成本是一个有效措施，但这也只是在较小程度减少而非消除了公司在流动性方面的危险性。（marginally）

_____

_____

4. 该公司一直通过商业杂志广告来扩展客户群，但效果始终不太理想。（expand）

_____

_____

5. 英国软件制造商 Micro Focus 的股价周一暴跌，原因是该公司发布的最新交易报告反响不佳，首席执行官辞职。（collapse）

_____

_____

Writing

 Write a report comparing the monthly sales of _Fresh 'n' Cool_ with those of the previous year.

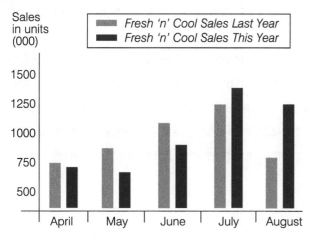

Business know-how

Read the following passage and make an oral summary of the main points to your partner or group.

Initial public offering (IPO)

Initial public offering (IPO) or stock market launch is a type of public offering in which shares of a company are sold to institutional investors and usually also retail (individual) investors; an IPO is underwritten (承销) by one or more investment banks, who also arrange for the shares to be listed on one or more stock exchanges. Through this process, colloquially known as floating, or going public, a privately held company is transformed into a public company. Initial public offerings can be used: to raise new equity capital for the company concerned; to monetise the investments of private shareholders such as company founders or private equity investors; and to enable easy trading of existing holdings or future capital raising by becoming publicly traded enterprises.

After the IPO, shares traded freely in the open market are known as the free float (自由流通股). Stock exchanges stipulate a minimum free float both in absolute terms (the total value as determined by the share price multiplied by the number of shares sold to the public) and as a proportion of the total share capital (i.e., the number of shares sold to the public divided by the total shares outstanding). Although IPO offers many benefits, there are also significant costs involved, chiefly those associated with the process such as banking and legal fees, and the ongoing requirement to disclose important and sometimes sensitive information.

Details of the proposed offering are disclosed to potential purchasers in the form of a lengthy document known as a prospectus (招股说明书). Most companies undertake an IPO with the assistance of an investment banking firm acting in the capacity of an underwriter. Underwriters provide several services, including help with correctly assessing the value of shares (share price) and establishing a public market for shares (initial sale). Alternative methods such as the Dutch auction (拍卖) have also been explored and applied for several IPOs.

The following extracts are from the CEO's statement in four annual reports.

`08 05 90 91 92 93 94 95 96 97 98 99 00 01`

a   Strike action and unfavourable exchange rates led to losses that were almost balanced by gains from our ongoing resource efficiency programme, which delivered an impressive £100m of cost performance improvements. Another source of revenue was the recent disposal of Dennox, our wholly-owned subsidiary.

b

The company made steady progress, with profits before tax and exceptional items increasing to £596m. Careful cash management continues to be a major feature of the company's strong performance. Despite pressures from increased investment activity, the balance sheet shows net cash at £3.2bn after expenditure of £346m.

c   Trading volume increased by 4.5%, which was well up on recent years, and turnover rose by 3%. Operating margins also increased, as a result of the restructuring programme that was completed at the end of last year. Although successful, the programme meant a reduction in net cash to £472m.

d   Our major achievement last year was the £4.8bn acquisition of a speciality chemicals business. This investment, along with the planned sale of assets, will help streamline the company's range of businesses. Trading profit fell by 7% due to disappointments in non-core activities, confirming the logic of the actions we are taking.

Words and expressions

asset /'æset/	**n.** 资产	**balance sheet**	收支平衡表；资产负债表
disposal /dɪ'spəʊzl/	**n.** 处理	**exchange rate**	汇率
expenditure /ɪk'spendɪtʃə(r)/	**n.** 支出	**net cash**	净现金；基本金额
reduction /rɪ'dʌkʃən/	**n.** 缩小；减少	**operating margin**	营业毛利
streamline /'striːmlaɪn/	**v.** 改进；使……简单化	**resource efficiency**	资源效益
strike /straɪk/	**n.** 罢工		

Comprehension tasks

 Read the text. Which extract does each sentence below refer to?

1. The company enjoyed a substantial increase in its sales.
2. The company offset some of its poor trading results by selling assets.
3. The CEO explains why substantial investment was necessary.
4. The CEO refers to the success of previous organisational changes.
5. The company's cost-cutting measures are proving very successful.
6. The CEO refers to the company's success in controlling new spending.
7. The company is currently implementing a major transformation programme.

 Read the extracts again. Underline words and phrases which link cause and effect. Think of other words and phrases you could use in their place.

Vocabulary

Match the sentence halves by use of linking lines.

1. We've just paid off the money that
2. There was an economic recession, which
3. We've got $15m of surplus stock, which
4. We didn't pay a dividend this year, which
5. They announced a $2.2bn profit, which
6. They recruited a new CEO, who
7. I invested in a company whose
8. The report's due in April, which

a. upset a lot of shareholders.
b. we borrowed from the bank in May.
c. shares have performed well all year.
d. caused their shares to rise by 12%.
e. badly affected our domestic sales.
f. is just sitting in our warehouse.
g. is the end of the financial year.
h. used to work for a main competitor.

Rewrite the sentences using relative clauses.

1. Many Internet companies started last year. They are now out of business.

   _____

2. They wrote off $400,000 of bad debts. They couldn't recover these debts.

   _____

3. Michael O'Leary is the CEO of Ryanair. Ryanair is a low-cost airline.

   _____

4. Nick Leeson was a trader. His dealings put Barings Bank out of business.

   _____

5. The figures didn't include tax. The tax makes a big difference.

   _____

Complete the web page with the correct prepositions.

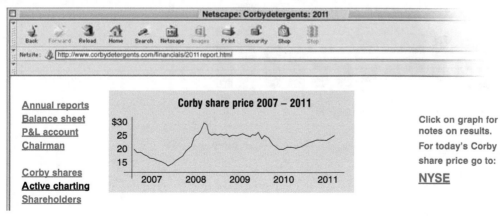

Press releases	Corby shares fell steadily in 2007 (1) _from_ $20 (2) _____ $15.
Contact	The following year saw shares shoot up (3) _____ $15 to reach
HOME	almost $30 in June before a slight fall (4) _____ $5 by the end of

Corby shares fell steadily in 2007 (1) _from_ $20 (2) _____ $15. The following year saw shares shoot up (3) _____ $15 to reach almost $30 in June before a slight fall (4) _____ $5 by the end of the year. The share price remained steady (5) _____ $25 throughout 2009 but then fell again (6) _____ around $4 to remain (7) _____ approximately $20 (8) _____ 2010. An improvement (9) _____ market conditions saw a steady increase (10) _____ the share price throughout 2011.

Speaking

Work in pairs. Describe the graph below to your partner.

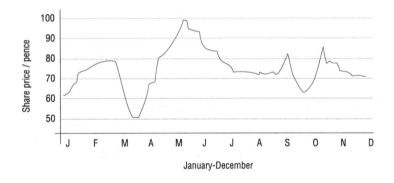

Work in pairs. Describe the bar chart below to your partner.

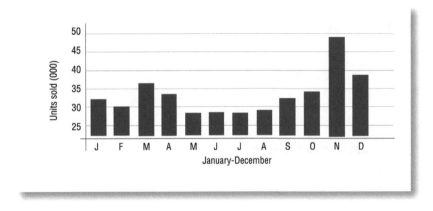

Business communication

TASK 8 Work in pairs. Suppose your company has a large cash surplus and wants to invest in shares. Look at the information about Ramsden Energy Drinks and Bute Chemicals plc. Which company would you invest in?

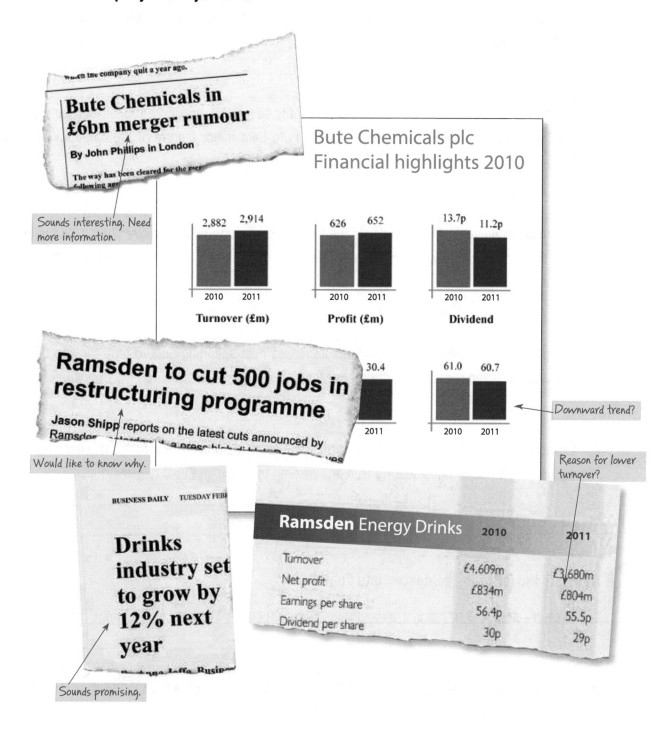

...ch the company quit a year ago.

Bute Chemicals in £6bn merger rumour

By John Phillips in London

The way has been cleared for the mer... following ag...

Sounds interesting. Need more information.

Bute Chemicals plc
Financial highlights 2010

2,882   2,914

| 2010 | 2011 |

Turnover (£m)

626   652

| 2010 | 2011 |

Profit (£m)

13.7p   11.2p

| 2010 | 2011 |

Dividend

Ramsden to cut 500 jobs in restructuring programme

Jason Shipp reports on the latest cuts announced by Ramsde...

Would like to know why.

30.4

2011

61.0   60.7

| 2010 | 2011 |

Downward trend?

Reason for lower turnover?

BUSINESS DAILY   TUESDAY FEB

Drinks industry set to grow by 12% next year

Sounds promising.

Ramsden Energy Drinks	2010	2011
Turnover	£4,609m	£3,680m
Net profit	£834m	£804m
Earnings per share	56.4p	55.5p
Dividend per share	30p	29p

Translation

 Translate the following sentences into Chinese.

1. Strike action and unfavourable exchange rates led to looses that were almost balanced by gains from our ongoing resource efficiency programme, which delivered an impressive £100m of cost performance improvements.

2. The company made steady progress, with profits before tax and exceptional items increasing to £596m. Careful cash management continues to be a major feature of the company's strong performance.

3. Our major achievement last year was the £4.8bn acquisition of a specialty chemicals business. This investment, along with the planned sale of assets, will help streamline the company's range of businesses.

4. The president has generally favoured tax increases over spending cuts to plug the gap between government revenue and expenditure, but the citizens obviously favoured the opposite.

5. Economic data published by Chinese provincial-level regions for the first half year show that economic restructuring is bearing fruit and leading to stable and quality growth.

Translate the following sentences into English.

1. 最近的一项研究证实了实际汇率失调和动荡对经济绩效的负面影响。（exchange rate）

2. IBM 明确表示，继去年夏天整合部分业务后，为了提高效率和竞争力，它需要继续精简公司结构。（streamline）

3. 由于经济形势好转，这家公司今年的年营业额增长了 15%，达到每年 4.5 万英镑。（turnover）

4. 掌握这项技术的 B2B 公司的股东回报率比其他公司高出 8%，年复合增长率（CAGR）是其他公司的 5 倍。（revenue）

5. 该公司提供可持续的塑料垃圾处理服务和解决方案，帮助企业和个人轻松处理塑料垃圾并实现环保目标。（disposal）

Writing

TASK 11 Write a report comparing the two companies in Task 8 and recommending the most suitable for investment. Before you write, please answer the following questions. Make notes and then write your report. Remember to give a recommendation.

- How many parts will the report have?
- Which information will come under each heading?
- What kind of expressions will you need?

UNIT 8 The future of work

Warming up

TASK 1 Compare the way people work before and after the invention of the Internet, and talk to your partner about it.

TASK 2 Think about how the ways of working might change in the future.

Text A   The future of work

    This is as good as it gets. The golden beach, the crystal clear water and the gentle refreshing breeze. You knew working from Sri Lanka for a few months would be a good idea, but this is paradise. Suddenly your pleasant thoughts are interrupted by your phone—the meeting, of course! Lying on the beach, you'd forgotten all about it.

    Quickly, you gather your things and head back to the rented beach house. You walk through the terrace doors and shout at your personal work organiser to download any mail and access all the meeting preparation files. On the wall a large flat monitor hums and flickers into life as you head into the shower. You walk back into the room to see your team leader's face on the wall giving details about the marketing project and today's objectives. You try to pinpoint exactly what it is about him that you dislike, but you can't. Not that it matters, of course, because in six weeks the project will be over and you'll probably never see his face on your wall again. Your work organiser has already scanned the web and applied for several new assignments. It knows what work you want to do and how much you expect to earn. It then does the rest for you—searching through the thousands of vacancies on the web and selecting those most compatible with your CV, which, of course, it updates automatically before submitting. You forget the briefing for a moment and gaze out across the terrace at the waves gently lapping against the shore. Did people really use to work in the same office all their lives?

Words and expressions

breeze /briːz/	n.	微风，轻风	terrace /'terəs/	n.	（房屋旁的）露台；草坪
briefing /'briːfɪŋ/	n.	简报；基本情况介绍会	crystal clear		清澈透明的
flicker /'flɪkə(r)/	v.	闪烁；闪光	CV (Curriculum Vitae)		简历
hum /hʌm/	v.	发低哼声	flat monitor		平板显示器
paradise /'pærədaɪz/	n.	天堂；乐园	gaze out		向外注视，眺望
refreshing /rɪ'freʃɪŋ/	adj.	提神的；清爽的	lap against		轻拍

Comprehension tasks

Read the text and note down the tools that help the author work and how they help.

Tools	Functions

Read the text again and judge whether the following statements are "Right" or "Wrong" according to the text. If there is not enough information to answer "Right" or "Wrong", write "Doesn't say".

1. The author is working in paradise now. _____

2. The author has flexible work hours and work places. _____

3. The work organizer could do all the work for the author, including preparing for files and attending meetings. _____

4. According to the work mode described in the text, the employees would have a permanent boss/team leader. _____

5. This work mode will challenge people's work efficiency and work ethics. _____

Vocabulary

 Choose the correct word to fill each gap.

Well, I've been here for a few months now and I'm really enjoying it. It's quite different from my last job. For one thing, the working (1) _____ here is definitely very different from the old company.

The managers have (2) _____ flexible working up the agenda and (3) _____ areas where it would make more (4) _____ to work from home. After all, if we are all (5) _____ onto the same network, then the (6) _____ of your workstation doesn't really matter, does it? It's just as easy to (7) _____ to a team using email and the telephone. Working from home is a win-win situation because it increases efficiency and cuts the time it (8) _____ travelling to the office.

1. a. style   b. surrounding   c. environment
2. a. pushed   b. encouraged   c. promoted
3. a. controlled   b. identified   c. clarified
4. a. sense   b. logic   c. value
5. a. joined   b. logged   c. booked
6. a. location   b. workplace   c. premises
7. a. connect   b. contribute   c. co-operate
8. a. lasts   b. demands   c. takes

TASK 4 Match the words by use of linking lines.

1. book ——————————— premises
2. foster \ a meeting room
3. key a number into operations
4. run out of a telephone terminal
5. show team spirit
6. centralise supplies
7. adapt to interest
8. vacate a new way of working

TASK 5 Complete each sentence with a suitable preposition.

1. There's a connection _____ lifestyle and performance in the workplace.
2. The use of email has a definite impact _____ things like formality in the office environment.
3. We're very dependent _____ the intranet, so if it goes down our operations are badly affected.
4. Some jobs, such as marketing, are more suited _____ flexible working than others.
5. I bumped _____ Sarah at the café this morning.
6. The company I'm working for now has even got a gym and a café _____ site.

Listening

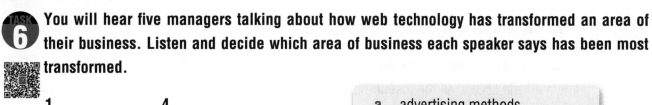

TASK 6 You will hear five managers talking about how web technology has transformed an area of their business. Listen and decide which area of business each speaker says has been most transformed.

1. _____   4. _____

2. _____   5. _____

3. _____

a. advertising methods
b. after-sales service
c. client information service
d. customer purchasing process
e. production processes
f. supply management
g. sales network
h. training methods

Listen to the recording again and fill in the table.

Speakers	Main benefit the speaker mentions
1	
2	
3	
4	
5	

Business communication

 Suppose your company is based in Beijing and is launching a remote working system that will change the way people work. You have been asked to introduce this system in the product launch. Discuss the following questions and give a launch product presentation in front of your class.

- What are the features of the remote working system?
- How will it benefit the way people work?
- Who are the potential buyers of the system?

Translation

Translate the following sentences into Chinese.

1. You walk through the terrace doors and shout at your personal work organiser to download any mail and access all the meeting preparation files. On the wall a large flat monitor hums and flickers into life as you head into the shower.

_____

_____

2. Your work organiser has already scanned the web and applied for several new assignments. It knows what work you want to do and how much you expect to earn.

_____

_____

3. It then does the rest for you—searching through the thousands of vacancies on the web and selecting those most compatible with your CV, which, of course, it updates automatically before submitting.

_____

_____

4. In terms of AI, Kai-Fu Lee thinks China will win because it has the edge in the four determinants of AI success: brains, capital, regulation and data. His verdict on the last three criteria is largely persuasive.

_____

_____

5. Whereas American cities are restricting self-driving cars, the district of Xiong'an, 60 miles south of Beijing, is being built from scratch to accommodate them (along with 2.5m people). The mayors of Chinese cities are splashing cash on AI startups.

_____

_____

TASK 10 **Translate the following sentences into English.**

1. 在招聘时，雇主应该明确指出申请者须具备何种技能，这样才能提高招聘的效率。(pinpoint)

_____

_____

2. 总经理让秘书在会议前把所有的会议资料扫描一份，并通过电子邮件发送给所有的参会代表。(scan)

_____

_____

3. 自从李明跳槽到一家全球 500 强企业之后，人力资源部经理一直想办法填补这个设计总监的空缺。(vacancy)

_____

_____

4. 公司的技术部正在为新开发的产品申请专利，以保护自己的知识产权。(apply for)

_____

_____

5. 为了应对最近的公关危机，公司正计划近期举行一个情况通报会，介绍一下公关情况的最新进展。(briefing)

_____

_____

Writing

Write a report on a company's website. Include information about the site's strengths and weakness and make recommendations for its further development.

Business know-how

Read the following passage and make an oral summary of the main points to your partner or group.

E-Business（电子商务）

The Internet is now used as a medium to conduct business, not only within the country, but around the world—thus the name World Wide Web (www). The common idea of engaging in a business venture is to have a particular store in which to sell or offer goods and services. However, the complexity of today's society demands more avenues（途径）through which that endeavour can actually be accomplished. Many modern-day entrepreneurs meet customer demands and offer goods and services through a method known as e-business.

E-business, or, in proper terms, electronic business, traces its roots from the use of the information superhighway, as a very effective means of conducting business endeavours. In 1997, IBM, one of the leading names in information technology, was the first to use the term when incorporating business endeavours toward a campaign emanating（发出）from that theme. As time goes on, the majority of businesses around the world are more inclined to use the Internet in the realisation of their goals for the company.

Aside from every transaction being conducted via the Internet, an e-business functions much like a conventional business, especially in the sense of supply and demand. The most basic, yet most important function to a successful e-business is good search engine optimisation（优化）. Search engine optimisation enables a web page to rank well in Google, MSN and other search-engine tools, thus allowing visitors and potential customers to easily and efficiently locate the site.

Five managers make predictions about the future of work.

Jeanne Desaill—Director, MAS

In future, work space will become less rigid, with hotdesking being the norm. People will expect a better standard of working environment too. There's likely to be more shift work, partly to make better use of office equipment but also to offer services around the clock. In fact, I think working hours will probably change quite dramatically. For instance, there'll be no guarantee of free time even at the weekend. Some of the business community worry that staff won't work unless supervised but the real issue will be recognising when staff are overtaxing themselves.

Joshua Golder—Institute of Employment Studies

People are beginning to make the connection between lifestyle, performance and sickness, so I think we're bound to see a move towards promoting lifestyle issues in the office. The banning of smoking in public places is one example of this. There'll also undoubtedly be a lot of larger companies realising the importance of their social obligations. Smart firms are already pushing these responsibilities up the agenda and showing a lot more interest in the needs of people in their immediate environment.

Megan O'Riordan—Client Director, Dewbury Newton Carter

In future, part-time staff may be working for one employer in the morning and a different one in the afternoon, so values and branding will definitely need to be stronger. Staff interaction will be through telecommunications rather than the place of work. However, technology such as email has an impact on things like style and formality and old courtesies tend to disappear. So one requirement for a healthy organisation is certainly going to be maintaining respect in relationships.

Janice Watson—Staffordshire Teleworking Community

Companies will have to concentrate more on establishing employee loyalty, which will be hard won, with many people preferring to improve their CVs and move on to another company rather than get stressed out in their current job. Another issue is that with the growth in teleworking, how are authorities going to cope when all their taxation systems depend entirely on location? There's also no longer any clear distinction between employed and self-employed and, the way things are going, this distinction is set to disappear altogether.

Sachin Kapur—Director, Cyber Office

With people working from anywhere, there'll be a great change in employee demands in terms of contractual arrangements and the lifestyles of working people. They'll demand a healthier balance between work and leisure as it becomes less obvious when work "stops". What I'm worried about, however, is the erosion of people's rights if they're working for a huge company where there's little personal communication. And on a more global scale, how will a single state control a multinational which has far more resources and a lot more money?

Words and expressions

branding /ˈbrændɪŋ/	n.	品牌化，品牌
erosion /ɪˈrəʊʒn/	n.	侵蚀，腐蚀
formality /fɔːˈmælətɪ/	n.	礼节；拘谨
hotdesking /ˌhɒtˈdeskɪŋ/	n.	办公桌共享
norm /nɔːm/	n.	标准，规范
overtax /ˌəʊvəˈtæks/	v.	使负担过重
rigid /ˈrɪdʒɪd/	adj.	僵硬的，死板的
supervise /ˈsuːpəvaɪz/	v.	监督，管理

telecommunication /ˌtelɪkəˌmjuːnɪˈkeɪʃən/	n.	电信
teleworking /ˈtelɪwɜːkɪŋ/	n.	远程工作
around the clock		夜以继日地，全天候
be bound to		必然；一定要
contractual agreement		契约协议
employee loyalty		员工忠诚度

Comprehension tasks

Match each statement below with one of the managers in the text.

1. People will work for more than one company at a time.

2. People will want to have more free time in the future.

3. There will be a lot more concern about health in the workplace.

4. As work becomes more flexible, people will work longer hours.

5. Governments will find it difficult to collect revenue from workers and companies.

6. Companies will have to ensure that communications remain polite.

7. Companies will be more closely involved with local communities.

8. Large organisations will become more powerful than some governments.

TASK 2 Read the text again. How many different ways of expressing predictions can you find? Put the predictions in order of strength.

_____

_____

_____

Vocabulary

TASK 3 Match the verbs with the appropriate nouns.

	a meeting	needs	time
save	X	X	✓
meet			
spend			
run			
predict			
suit			
hold			
waste			

TASK 4 Complete the crossword.

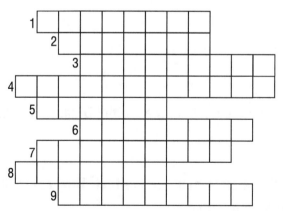

1. E-business is using _____ technology to transform basic business processes.
2. Most large companies now have a _____ where customers can access product information.

3. The Internet is very flexible and allows companies to update their news _____ very quickly.

4. Many people worry about using credit cards to make financial _____ over the Internet.

5. More and more people are getting connected to the Internet and then buying goods _____.

6. Many large companies have a secure company-wide computer network called an _____.

7. The challenge is to _____ Internet technologies into the company's business processes.

8. In order to access the World Wide Web, you need to use a web _____.

9. Companies have to remember that e-business is about _____ and not technology.

TASK 5 Use the exact form of the word in the bracket to rewrite each prediction.

1. Traffic congestion could be eased by teleworking.
   (may) Teleworking may ease traffic congestion.

2. I can't imagine the office will cease to be important.
   (unlikely) _____

3. It looks as if the Internet's ready to explode.
   (set) _____

4. More people will want to work from home.
   (bound) _____

5. I don't think everyone will have an iPad®.
   (improbable) _____

6. Working from home is sure to increase in future.
   (undoubtedly) _____

Speaking

TASK 6 Look at the five statements in the text. Which of them do you agree with? Discuss it with your partner.

TASK 7 Work in pairs. Discuss the merits of each of these statements in the text. How could they be changed to make them better reflect good working practice?

Business communication

8 Use the Internet to find out about shared office space and make a presentation about the pros and cons of office sharing.

Translation

9 Translate the following sentences into Chinese.

1. Some of the business community worry that staff won't work unless supervised but the real issue will be recognising when staff are overtaxing themselves.

   _____

   _____

2. Smart firms are already pushing these responsibilities up the agenda and showing a lot more interest in the needs of people in their immediate environment.

   _____

   _____

3. Companies will have to concentrate more on establishing employee loyalty, which will be hard won, with many people preferring to improve their CVs and move on to another company rather than get stressed out in their current job.

_____

_____

4. More recently, many airlines have introduced in-flight entertainment services that can be accessed on passenger smartphones via the aircraft's Wi-Fi system. Could the next step in the evolution of in-flight entertainment be virtual-reality goggles?

_____

_____

5. For airlines, the potential of virtual reality is attractive, too. People on business trips could imagine that they are on the beach or in the mountains, rather than hemmed into a tightly packed flying tube.

_____

_____

TASK 10 Translate the following sentences into English.

1. 精准快速的物流系统、全天候的在线客户服务为网站带来了超高的人气，令这个新兴的购物网站在众多竞争对手中脱颖而出。(around the clock)

_____

_____

2. 近几年，我国在转变政府职能、深化监管体制改革方面取得了很大进展。在肯定成绩的同时，也要清醒地看到，政府监管体系还存在一些问题。(supervise)

_____

_____

3. 该公司去年采用了远程办公系统，一年来公司的工作效率大大提高，员工的工作时间也更为灵活。(teleworking)

_____

_____

4. 根据工会的调查，该工厂大约有 60% 的工人每周都在从事不同类型的轮班工作，而且经常加班。(shift work)

_____

_____

5. 在人员流动性越来越强的社会，如何提高员工忠诚度、如何留住人才是让很多公司头疼的问题。(employee loyalty)

_____

_____

TASK 11 Look at the graph showing the predicted growth of online and web-influenced retail sales. Write a report comparing online retail sales and in-store sales influenced by websites with total retail sales.

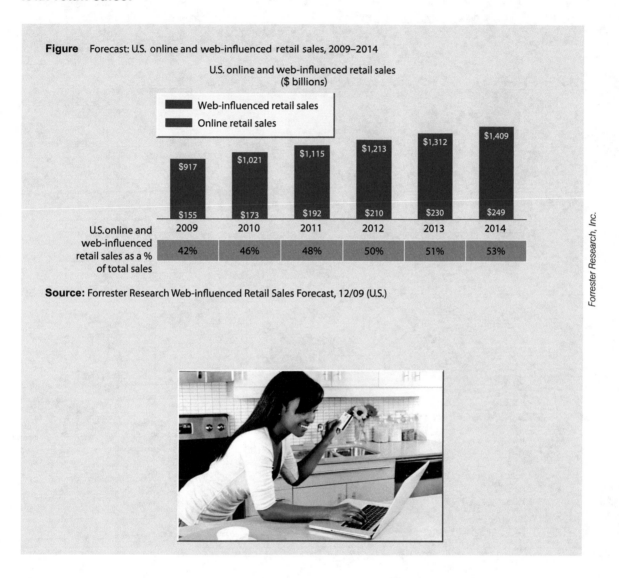

Figure Forecast: U.S. online and web-influenced retail sales, 2009–2014

U.S. online and web-influenced retail sales ($ billions)

- Web-influenced retail sales
- Online retail sales

	2009	2010	2011	2012	2013	2014
Web-influenced retail sales	$917	$1,021	$1,115	$1,213	$1,312	$1,409
Online retail sales	$155	$173	$192	$210	$230	$249
U.S. online and web-influenced retail sales as a % of total sales	42%	46%	48%	50%	51%	53%

Source: Forrester Research Web-influenced Retail Sales Forecast, 12/09 (U.S.)

Forrester Research, Inc.

Case study

Globalisation

Warming up

TASK 1 Think of three successful products. Why are they successful?

TASK 2 Put each of the three products in the appropriate quarter of the framework below. Which products are most suitable for globalisation?

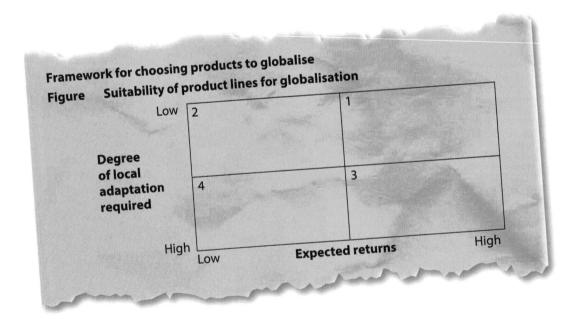

Framework for choosing products to globalise
Figure   Suitability of product lines for globalisation

	Low		
	2		1
Degree of local adaptation required			
	4		3
	High		

Low   Expected returns   High

The Marriott Corporation had been in the hotel business for about thirty years when the management decided they needed to become an international company. It was therefore necessary to decide on a strategy of globalisation.

Marriott.

As the company began its globalisation, it had to decide which product lines to start with. The figure (on the previous page) represents a framework to identify those product lines suitable for early globalisation. As indicated, each line of business in the company's portfolio should be evaluated along two dimensions—potential pay-off (expected returns) and potential risk (degree of local adaptation required).

The first dimension focuses on the potential profits of globalisation. In Marriott's case, the two products with the highest margins were its full-service hotels (the "Marriott" brand) and long-term-stay hotels (the "Residence Inn" brand). In a business such as the Marriott hotels, where the principal customers are globetrotting corporate executives, a worldwide presence can create significant value because the company can use a centralised reservations system and develop globally standardised services which assure customers of high quality.

The second dimension refers to the level of adaptation required to enter foreign markets. Since any new development involves risk, the greater the degree of local adaptation required,

the greater the risk of failure. For the Marriott Corporation, both its "Marriott" and "Courtyard" brands could successfully offer globally standardised services, whereas the retirement communities and the long-term-stay hotels would require far more local adaptation.

Thus, full-service hotels offered both a greater pay-off and less risk and seemed to be the best candidate for globalisation.

However, since Marriott began to expand internationally, the "Courtyard" brand has become more popular in the international market. It proved to be an extremely adaptable brand and the management team quickly realised that offering ergonomic work space, Internet access, business libraries and 24-hour food service would attract business travellers around the globe. The marketing strategy of billing it as "The business hotel designed by business travellers, for business travellers" has certainly paid off. The cost of staying at a Courtyard is lower than the upscale Marriott hotels, but being a high volume product has greatly improved the returns on the brand.

Words and expressions

adaptation /ˌædæp'teɪʃən/	*n.*	适应；调整	
bill /bɪl/	*v.*	宣传；宣布	
dimension /daɪ'menʃən/	*n.*	维度	
ergonomic /ˌɜːgə'nɒmɪk/	*adj.*	人体工程学的	
evaluate /ɪ'væljʊeɪt/	*v.*	衡量；评价	

globetrotting /'gləʊbtrɒtɪŋ/	*adj.*	环游世界的
pay-off /'peɪɒf/	*n.*	回报
portfolio /ˌpɔːt'fəʊlɪəʊ/	*n.*	（业务、产品等）组合
standardised /'stændədaɪzd/	*adj.*	标准化的
upscale /'ʌpskeɪl/	*adj.*	高级的，高档的

Comprehension tasks

 Read the text and answer the following questions.

1. What should the company decide first before it begins its globalisation?
2. Why can the worldwide presence of Marriott hotels create significant value?
3. How are local adaptation and risk of failure related?
4. What kind of hotels seemed to be the best candidate for globalisation?
5. In what way has the "Courtyard" brand become more popular in the international market?

 Read the text again. Put these Marriott brands into the framework.

- "Marriott" brand (full-service hotels)
- "Courtyard" brand (mid-price hotels)
- "Residence Inn" brand (long-term-stay hotels)
- Marriott Senior Living Services (retirement communities)

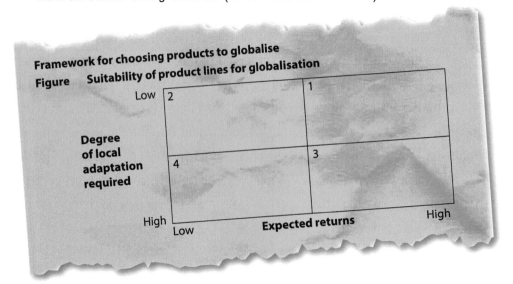

Framework for choosing products to globalise
Figure   Suitability of product lines for globalisation

Vocabulary

3 Complete the word diagram with the following marketing words and phrases.

subscription	free sample	flood	exhibition	outlets	dominate
sponsorship	chain stores	media	saturate	boom	franchise
direct selling	word of mouth	TV adverts	break into		

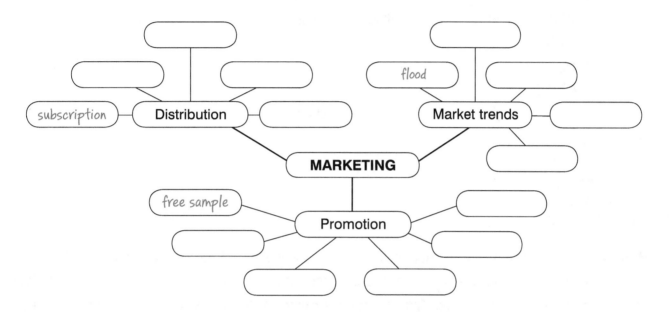

4 Match the words with the definitions by use of linking lines.

1. positioning
2. mark-up
3. margin
4. loss-leader
5. franchise
6. mailshot
7. gimmick
8. point of sale
9. marketing mix

a. sell another company's goods under strict guidelines
b. placing of a product in a market (price, image, etc.)
c. strategic combination of product, price, place and promotion
d. something to attract attention to a product
e. place where a product is actually sold
f. difference between selling price and cost of production
g. amount of profit a product makes
h. product sold without profit to gain market share
i. generation of new business with a postal promotion

TASK 5 Which word does not go with the word in capital letters?

1. MARKETING
   plan   (lifestyle)   mix   strategy

2. PRODUCT
   position   withdraw   launch   saturate

3. MARKET
   black   target   billboard   free

4. DIRECT
   marketing   mail   selling   slogan

5. PRESS
   prospectus   conference   release   launch

6. MARKET
   leader   jingle   value   share

Listening

TASK 6 IKEA is a multinational company founded in Sweden in 1943. The company designs and sells ready-to-assemble furniture and accessories, and operates over 300 no frill furniture stores in over 35 countries. The Managing Director of IKEA U.K. talks about the company's corporate culture. Listen and choose one letter for the correct answer.

1. How alike are all IKEA's stores worldwide?

   a. Each store has the same management practices.

   b. Each store carries a different product range.

   c. Each store is adapted to the local culture.

2. What was the main influence on the formation of IKEA's values?

   a. Traditional Swedish values.

   b. Ingvar Kamprad's personal values.

   c. Different cultural values within IKEA.

3. IKEA can cope with the diversity of its workforce because

   a. its managers have international experience.

   b. its basic corporate values are found in all cultures.

   c. its employees interpret IKEA's beliefs differently.

4. What is the main advantage of a strong corporate culture?

   a. It makes international transfers easier.

b. It reduces the cost of global marketing.

c. It stops competitors copying IKEA.

5. What is IKEA's main policy for educating its staff?

   a. It produces educational videos and brochures.

   b. It holds special training sessions for managers.

   c. It encourages regular meetings to discuss culture.

6. How does IKEA's culture affect its recruitment process?

   a. Candidates are assessed on their personal qualities.

   b. Highly skilled candidates are attracted to vacancies.

   c. Candidates from a retail background are preferred.

7. What role does culture play in promotion decisions at IKEA?

   a. Only Swedes can become senior managers.

   b. A knowledge of Swedish culture is vital for promotion.

   c. Nationality plays no part in promotion decisions.

8. Since the mid-1980s, IKEA's development has been most affected by the

   a. stepping down of Ingvar Kamprad as President.

   b. challenge of increasingly competitive markets.

   c. way it has expanded over the last ten years.

TASK 7 **Listen to the interview again and complete the sentences with the missing words and phrases.**

1. Although our culture will naturally _____ the local culture to some extent, our core values such as simplicity and cost-consciousness are _____ in all cultures.

2. Well, they have evolved over the last fifty-seven years, of course, but I think our _____ "A better life for the majority of people" still very much reflects the _____ of those early years.

3. And from a marketing and _____ point of view it's very advantageous as well. But the real _____ is that it makes IKEA unique.

4. Videos and _____ are helpful tools but only if used in conjunction with "_____" and discussing values with management.

5. It would be impossible, however, for anyone to _____ within IKEA without wholly understanding and _____ the company's philosophy and culture.

Business communication

8 Look at the three aspects of a brand as illustrated below. Which aspects of the following brands do you think are global?

| Coca-Cola | Mars | Hertz | Nike | Barilla | Nescafé |

Concept, promise or benefit

Name, trademarks, symbols and logo

Products and services

Translation

9 Translate the following sentences into Chinese.

1. In a business such as the Marriott hotels, where the principal customers are globetrotting corporate executives, a worldwide presence can create significant value because the company can use a centralised reservations system and develop globally standardised services which assure customers of high quality.

2. Both brands could successfully offer globally standardised services, whereas the retirement communities and the long-term-stay hotels would require far more local adaptation. Thus, full-service hotels offered both a greater pay-off and less risk and seemed to be the best candidate for globalisation.

3. The marketing strategy of billing it as "The business hotel designed by business travellers, for business travellers" has certainly paid off. The cost of staying at a Courtyard is lower than the up-scale Marriott hotels, but being a high volume product has greatly improved the returns on the brand.

4. Multinational companies will continue to find opportunities for expansion and will face new obstacles to the sustainability of their investments. In this era of guarded globalisation, however, both are likely to be moving targets that will require constant strategic adaptation.

_____

_____

5. Private enterprises' rise was the highlight of China "Go Global" era 3.0, as they directly invested in foreign markets, set up factories overseas, employed local labour, and acquired foreign companies and infrastructure.

_____

_____

TASK 10 **Translate the following sentences into English.**

1. 产品组合的管理是整个商业战略中最重要的因素之一，因为它帮助公司达成整体商业目标，并且由此规划未来的产品线。它也是公司财务规划的重要工具。(portfolio)

_____

_____

2. 尽管跨国公司高管避免公开谈论这个话题，全球市场的利润却是不尽如人意——开展国际业务充满着不可预计的风险。即使对于最成功的那些跨国公司来说，国际市场的利润空间也比国内市场平均要低。(margin)

_____

_____

3. 中国的支付宝通过向与数字化连接的游客提供服务建立起全球业务。它提供的移动支付平台拥有 4 500 万活跃用户，支付宝被用作类似于信用卡的另一种选择。如今国外的高端百货公司、零售商以及知名国际品牌都支持用支付宝进行支付。(up-scale)

_____

_____

4. 美国公众长期以来对国际贸易都持怀疑态度，但是经济学家们表现得更为支持。然而，经济学文献中的新证据引发了关于如何评价贸易协定的新一轮思考。(evaluate)

_____

_____

5. 公司可以制定一系列的产品开发战略。有时公司根据每个市场定制产品，有时它们在所有地方都提供标准化产品，而有时它们会让步然后折中。(standardised)

_____

_____

Writing

TASK 11 Use the Internet to find out about a global brand that has adapted its products to a local market. Write a report on the case, analysing the strengths and weaknesses of its product strategy and what else could be done.

Business know-how

Read the following passage and illustrate the importance of globalisation orally to your partner.

Globalisation is a combination of the words "globalisation" and "localisation". The term is used to describe a product or service that is developed and distributed globally but is also adjusted to accommodate the user or consumer in a local market.

A global product or service, something everyone needs, may be tailored to conform with local laws, customs, or consumer preferences. Products that are "glocalised" are, by definition, going to be of much greater interest to the end user, the person who ends up using the product. It's localisation that makes the products more specific to an individual, their context, and their needs.

A common example would be cars that are sold worldwide but adjusted to meet local criteria such as emissions standards or what side the steering wheel is located. It could also focus on more cultural aspects, such as a global fast-food chain offering geographically-specific menu items that cater to local tastes. While globalisation helps customise an international corporation's products to a particular culture or geography, it must also pay attention to the risk of perceived cultural appropriation.

Globalisation works for companies with decentralised authority structures, and for companies that exist and compete in multiple, different cultural contexts. The process can be expensive, and resource intensive, but it often pays off for companies that practice it, as it allows for greater access to a larger, more culturally varied target market. It also makes companies more effective competitors in those markets.

Analysis Entering the market

Donald Fraser, a consultant at Kennedy, McLeish & Partners (KMP), talks about advising companies on exporting.

I = Interviewer **D** = Donald

I Donald, your consultancy helps companies enter foreign markets. What kind of help are companies looking for when they come to KMP?

D Well, companies usually have a specific market in mind and a pretty good idea as to which products they intend to export. But what they're not sure about is how to get the product into the target market.

I So what is the best way?

D Well, there are many options, from franchises to wholly-owned subsidiaries. The higher the degree of ownership, the more control you have. However, ownership also means more investment and, therefore, more risk.

I So what's the safest way of entering a market?

D Well, if you want to keep financial risk to a minimum, you should think about a licensing arrangement or perhaps a franchise. That way you don't have any of the costs associated with setting up production facilities. And, of course, you retain control of the product, which means you avoid some of the conflicts involved in joint ventures.

I But joint ventures are a very popular way of entering foreign markets.

D Yes, they are, because they allow a company to share some of the costs and risk. And even more importantly, they provide essential local knowledge without the cost of having to acquire a company. But they're not risk-free.

I So, what are the dangers of joint ventures?

D Well, in a typical joint venture the two partners pool their know-how and learn from each other as they work together. But, in fact, it's actually a learning race. One firm might learn much faster than the other and start taking all the decisions. It could eventually decide it has no more use for the arrangement and even terminate it.

I So, if you wanted to keep control and avoid that, a wholly-owned subsidiary would be the best option, then?

D It really depends on the target market. If, say, there's potentially a very high demand, then it would make sense to buy or set up a subsidiary and produce locally, because of economies of scale. Distance, of course, is another factor. Shipping to the other side of the world can be very expensive. That's why a lot of Japanese companies produce in Europe.

I   And what other factors can improve a company's chance of success?

D   Well, as I said, our clients usually know which products they want to export, but they often don't realise how much their product needs to be adapted. You see, some products require an understanding of local needs and an ability to use this knowledge in the product's design.

I   OK. So, let's say a company has successfully entered a market. How quickly should it look to expand?

D   Well, once again, it's finding the best way of minimising risk while optimising opportunity. However, under certain circumstances, a company is forced to expand in order to survive.

I   And when is this the case?

D   When, for example, you enter a market with a successful formula that's easy to copy—because you'll soon have a lot of local competitors offering the same products or services. Now, unless you're in a position to expand quickly enough to make economies of scale possible, these local companies will soon undercut you and price you out of the market.

I   And how can a company prepare for this expansion?

D   Well, the key to expansion is not spreading your managerial and financial resources too thinly. That's why it's crucial to develop a long-term strategy and make a thorough assessment of all the resources available for expansion.

Words and expressions

adapt /əˈdæpt/	*v.* 使适应		**pool** /puːl/	*v.* 聚集
consultancy /kənˈsʌltənsɪ/	*n.* 顾问工作；顾问服务公司		**terminate** /ˈtɜːmɪneɪt/	*v.* 停止，使终止
franchise /ˈfræntʃaɪz/	*n.* 特许经营		**undercut** /ˌʌndəˈkʌt/	*v.* 压低价
licensing /ˈlaɪsənsɪŋ/	*n.* 批准，准许		**economies of scale**	规模经济
minimise /ˈmɪnɪmaɪz/	*v.* 最小化		**financial risk**	财务风险
optimise /ˈɒptɪmaɪz/	*v.* 最优化		**make sense**	有意义；是明智的
option /ˈɒpʃən/	*n.* 选择		**target market**	目标市场

Comprehension tasks

Read the text and choose the best option to complete each sentence.

1. Companies approach KMP for advice on choosing

    a. the right products to export.

    b. the most suitable foreign market.

c. the best way of entering a market.

2. The safest method for a company to enter a foreign market is

   a. having an agreement with a local company.

   b. setting up its own local production.

   c. finding a joint venture partner.

3. The main advantage of joint ventures is that

   a. they are the cheapest way of entering a market.

   b. they are a risk-free way of doing business.

   c. they provide important market knowledge.

4. The danger with a joint venture is that one company might

   a. refuse to share know-how with the other partner.

   b. use the arrangement as the basis for a takeover.

   c. exploit and then leave the other partner.

5. A subsidiary is the best way of entering a market when

   a. high sales volumes are expected.

   b. the products are cheap to produce.

   c. a foreign market is near home.

6. Companies can improve their chances of success by

   a. developing new products exclusively for the market.

   b. changing the product to suit the target market.

   c. using designers recruited from the target market.

7. A company is forced to expand quickly when

   a. cheaper competition appears on the market.

   b. it has a successful formula that sells well.

   c. its production costs are very high.

8. Donald advises companies to prepare for expansion by

   a. training their key managers.

   b. having a comprehensive business plan.

   c. assessing their financial resources.

TASK 2 **Read the text again. What are the advantages and disadvantages of the following ways of entering a market?**

Franchise	Joint venture	Wholly-owned subsidiary
lower financial risk	can share costs and risks	complete control

Vocabulary

 Use the words to write sentences with *market*.

We need advice on entering our target market.

Russian

global   export

enter   target

consumer   (market)   knowledge

local   share

grow   report

presence

 Complete the table and then use the words to complete the sentences below.

verb	noun
promote	*promotion*
publicise	_____
_____	launch
license	_____
_____	feedback
differentiate	_____
position	_____
_____	campaign

1. We're going to run a big press ___*promotion*___ in three national newspapers.
2. We're trying hard to _____ our products from competitors' similar offerings.
3. They had a lot of bad _____ in the papers about the safety of the product.
4. We're launching a new TV advertising _____ next week.
5. It's vital we _____ the product properly. It has to be seen as better quality than the cheaper brands but offering the same quality as the more expensive ones.
6. We got some great _____ from the marketing questionnaires.
7. We don't want to set up an expensive overseas production facility so we're going to _____ a local manufacturer to produce the goods in the U.S.
8. The new product's having its official _____ on May 25 at a top New York hotel.

Which word in each group is the odd one out?

1. brochure   prospectus   advertisement   (report)
2. discounted   complimentary   free   gratis
3. product   performance   price   positioning
4. jingle   slogan   packaging   tune
5. trade mark   copyright   patent   logo
6. end-user   consumer   retailer   customer
7. merchandise   franchise   goods   products
8. dominate   break into   penetrate   enter

Speaking

Work in pairs. Discuss the following questions.

1. How can a worldwide presence add value to a company?
2. What are the risks involved in adapting a product for a foreign market?
3. What needs to be taken into account when adapting a brand to an international market?

Work in pairs. Discuss the major exports of your country and the companies involved in this business. Talk about how businesses decide what to export and if they sell the same products in their home markets.

Business communication

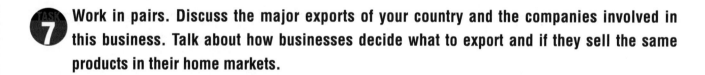

Work in pairs. Suppose your company is considering launching a new healthcare product. They are interested in selling to both men and women and are looking into marketing strategies to reach both groups. You have been asked to come up with marketing ideas. Discuss the situation together and decide:

- where to advertise the product and what type of promotions to do;
- where to sell the product.

Translate the following sentences into Chinese.

1. If you want to keep financial risk to a minimum, you should think about a licensing arrangement or perhaps a franchise. That way you don't have any of the costs associated with setting up production facilities.

2. In a typical joint venture the two partners pool their know-how and learn from each other as they work together. But one firm might learn much faster than the other and start taking all the decisions. It could eventually decide it has no more use for the arrangement and even terminate it.

3. When you enter a market with a successful formula that's easy to copy, unless you're in a position to expand quickly enough to make economies of scale possible, these local companies will soon undercut you and price you out of the market.

4. Many leading American digital firms, including Google, Amazon, eBay, and Uber, have successfully expanded internationally by introducing their products, services, and platforms in other countries. However, they have all failed in China, the world's largest digital market.

5. Going global has a number of advantages, but they do not come without challenges. If you can create an effective strategy for getting over the difficulties that globalisation might present, the process can reap many benefits that your business will get to enjoy for years into the future.

Translate the following sentences into English.

1. 花时间真正了解新客户十分重要。许多企业高管在开设海外子公司之前都会前往新市场，亲自观察新客户。你也可以聘请市场调研公司对新目标市场进行研究。(target market)

2. 通用电气感到应该在欧洲投入更多的企业基础设施及资源，既为了吸引、培养和保留最佳的欧洲员工，也为了政治上的原因让自己显得更"欧洲"。(retain)

3. 国际合资企业能带来诱人的机遇，但执行结果却往往不尽如人意。他们为什么会陷入困境？合作企业和管理人员又该怎样尽可能地提高成功的机率呢？（joint venture）

4. 规模经济是专业化和劳动分工的自然产物，是经济增长的主要动力之一。但是，企业不能永远实现规模经济。(economies of scale)

5. 每一场会议都应该有明确的议程，并实现重复的最小化，参会人员应该做好充分准备。办事高效的首席执行官会把这样的会议规范传播到整个组织。(minimise)

Writing

TASK 11 Suppose you work for Dayton, Inc. Look at the marketing information and handwritten notes. Write a report summarising the information and recommend action.

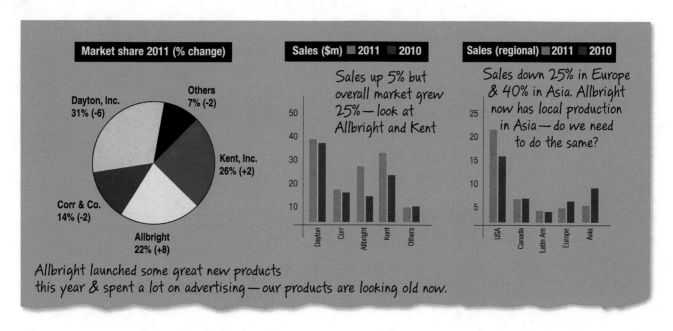

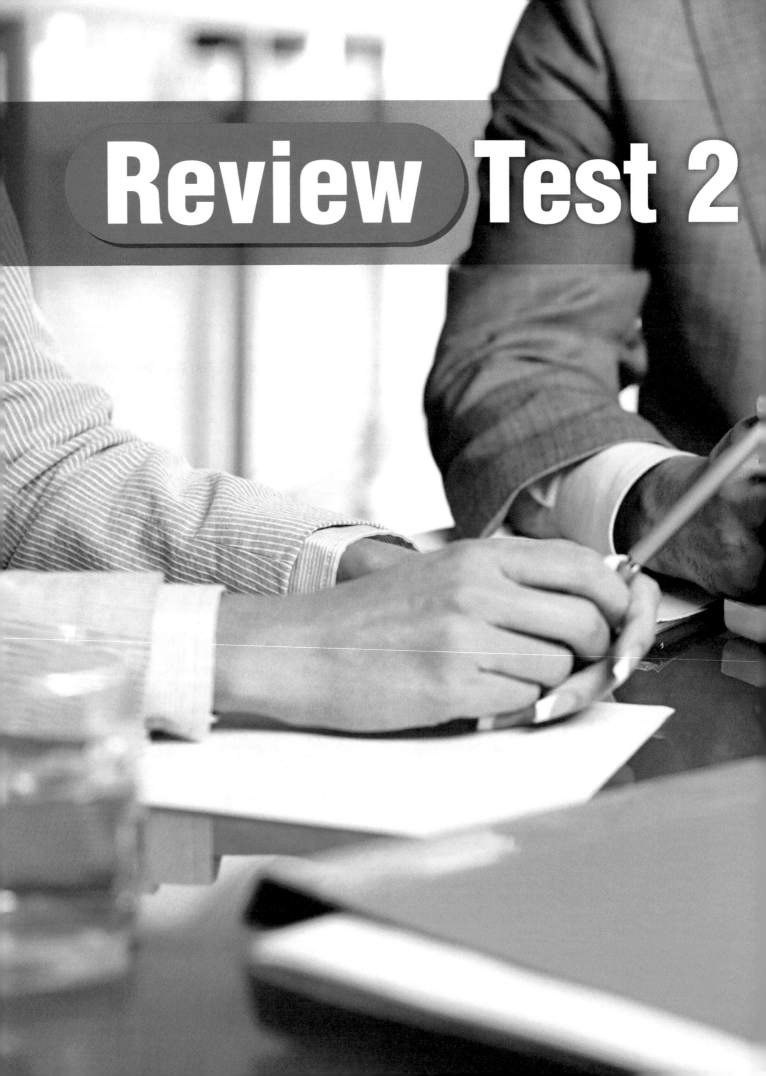

Part I

Listening comprehension

TASK 1 **Listen to the recording and for each question, mark one letter a, b, c or d.**

1. The main reason why ZSV introduced the flexible working scheme was
   a. to cope with social changes.
   b. to respond to market forces.
   c. to integrate new employees.
   d. to experiment on the latest office technology.

2. Most staff join the scheme to dedicate more time to their
   a. children.
   b. hobbies.
   c. education.
   d. career.

3. Sally thinks the most popular element of the scheme will be
   a. flexible hours.
   b. job-sharing.
   c. extended leave.
   d. compensation.

4. Most teleworkers keep in contact by using
   a. email facilities.
   b. the telephone.
   c. video-conferencing.
   d. voicemail.

5. Employees are selected for teleworking after an assessment of their
   a. home environment.
   b. job description.
   c. personal qualities.
   d. education background.

TASK 2 **Listen to the recording and fill in the missing information in each of the blanks.**

1. Management policies will determine how a company _____ all aspects of its business.

2. Without a coherent ethics policy, a company is in danger of surrendering a _____ to its rivals.

3. Only when the core values underpinning its _____ is identified, can a company develop new policies.

4. Ethical code is effective because it provides a clear understanding of what behavior is expected when employees are _____ with dilemmas.

5. In times of crisis, companies may not be able to avoid the damaging _____ simply by acting in an ethical manner.

 Listen to the recording and answer the following three questions.

1. What is globalisation all about, according to the first speaker?

2. What does the second speaker see as the main threats to national culture?

3. Why does the third speaker think India might benefit from globalisation?

Part II   Reading and writing

 Read the following article and choose the correct answer for each blank from a, b and c.

"Buying the market" is an arrangement whereby companies publish component (1) _____ and ask pre-qualified vendors to bid for the contract. It is a short-term deal with almost no (2) _____ with the supplier and the length of the bidding process is (3) _____ by half. Furthermore, the cost of order (4) _____ falls to around $5 an order as (5) _____ to $50 when it is done on paper. For companies such as aircraft manufacturer Boeing, (6) _____, such an arrangement with its engine suppliers would be unsuitable because of the complex (7) _____ between the body of the aircraft and its engines. For companies like Boeing, strategic (8) _____ make far more sense because they allow the company to work (9) _____ with its supplier, developing the aircraft's engines together. An added (10) _____ of this collaboration is that it reduces the financial risks of development programmes.

1. a. standards   **b.** specifications   **c.** criteria

2. a. exchange   **b.** feedback   **c.** communication

3. a. decreased   **b.** reduced   **c.** limited

4. a. processing   **b.** developing   **c.** delivering

5. a. contrary   **b.** opposed   **c.** different

6. a. although   **b.** nevertheless   **c.** however

7. a. structure   **b.** interaction   **c.** collaboration

8. a. relationships   **b.** alliances   **c.** arrangements

9. a. closely   **b.** precisely   **c.** mutually

10. a. potential   **b.** satisfaction   **c.** benefit

TASK 5 Read the graphs below. For each graph, there are one or two questions that follow. Choose the best answer from the four choices marked a, b, c and d.

Question 1 is based on the following graph.

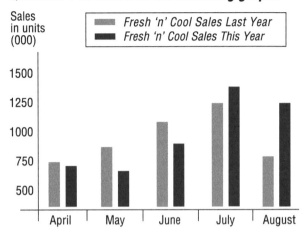

1. Which of the statements is NOT true?

   a. The graph compares the product sales of two years.

   b. This year's monthly sales is more than that of last year.

   c. The biggest sales of the product come in July.

   d. In April, the two years' sales are close to each other.

Questions 2–3 are based on the following graph about the share price of two companies.

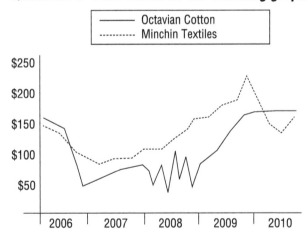

2. When does the share price of two companies decrease at the same time?

   a. 2006.　　　　　b. 2007.　　　　　c. 2008.　　　　　d. 2010.

3. Which of the statements is true?

   a. The share price of the two companies never goes hand in hand with each other.

   b. The share price of Octavian Cotton remains more stable.

   c. In 2009, Minchin Textiles reaches its peak of share price.

   d. The graph shows the share price of two companies in 10 years.

Questions 4–5 are based on the following graph.

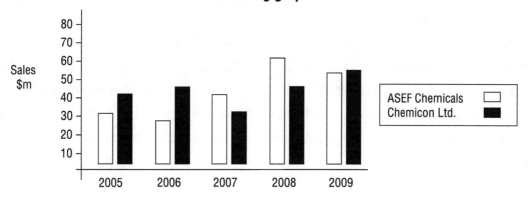

4. When does the sales of ASEF Chemicals begin to surpass that of Chemicon Ltd.?

   a. 2006.   b. 2007.   c. 2008.   d. 2009.

5. Which of the statements is true?

   a. The sales of the two companies have never go beyond 50 million.

   b. The sales of ASEF Chemicals grow steadily every year.

   c. In 2008, their sales are almost the same.

   d. The highest sales of the two companies is around 60 million.

Read the following two passages. Choose the best answer to each question.

Questions 1–8 are based on Passage 1.

Passage 1

a

Taler to cut U.K. workforce

Taler Chemicals, the Anglo-German industrial chemical company, announced yesterday that it is to cut 600 blue-collar jobs in a series of downsizing measures at three of its British plants. The news coincided with confirmation that the company also plans to dispose of its loss-making operations, CapPaints, the industrial solvent and paint division. This restructuring comes as the company reported a sharp drop in pre-tax profits. According to a company spokesman, the proposed joint venture with DTR International, one of Taler Chemicals' main competitors, is likely to be shelved.

b

Merger creates Hungarian software powerhouse

Silcom has finalised merger terms with ARER to create one of Hungary's largest computer software companies. Details of the merger are expected to be released later today. However, it is believed that Silcom's plans to break into France and Germany have been put on hold for the time being and that major job losses will soon be announced. Silcom looks set to benefit from the merger with ARER, which has recently been awarded a number of major contracts, including a contract with the Hungarian Ministry for Foreign Affairs, which will be worth in excess of $345,000 for the company.

Profit warning at LYT International

LYT International, one of Europe's leading Management Training Organisations, has warned shareholders to expect a fall in full year profits. The company, whose flagship training centre in Copenhagen is currently being modernised and refurbished, made an interim profit of $12m, compared with $23m in 2009. In response to its poor financial results, LYT has announced plans to cut jobs in its French and Spanish centres. An employee spokesman said that the move would prove unpopular and that with insufficient employees, some centres would struggle to deliver the high level of service demanded.

d

Shake-up at BTED

Nina Rantanen, former government adviser and the new CEO at BTED Power in Finland, has announced cost-cutting measures at the company. This decision has already led to the resignation of one of the company's most respected employees. Annika Ehlers had been with BTED Power for over twenty years, most recently as its Head of Operations. It is believed that she objected to company plans to reduce staffing levels at two of BTED Power's plants. Indications are that further high level resignations will follow in the next few months.

e

Restructuring plans announced at San Freight

San Freight has responded to redundancy rumours by revealing that it is to cut the number of office-based staff employed in its Scandinavian division by 25 percent over the next twenty-four months. The announcement follows confirmation that the company has also decided to postpone the planned upgrading of haulage systems at its Stockholm subsidiary. A senior staff member has revealed that San Freight's business has deteriorated in recent months due to the escalating price war with central and eastern European rivals.

Read the sentences below and the five news bulletins above. Which bulletin does each sentence refer to? For each sentence 1–8, mark one letter a, b, c, d or e. You will need to use some of the letters more than once.

1. This company will be working with a government organisation.
2. This company's decision to restructure will result in staff shortages.
3. This company is to reduce the number of administrative posts.
4. This company will sell off assets to offset poor financial results.
5. This company has made cuts which are unpopular with senior staff.
6. This company is in the process of upgrading some of its facilities.
7. This company has postponed its entry into new western European markets.
8. This company is suffering from the effects of increased competition.

Questions 9–14 are based on Passage 2.

Passage 2

Health and Safety Guidelines—Visual Display Units (VDUs)

In order to eliminate risk to the health and safety of employees, appliances should be used in accordance with suppliers' and manufacturers' instructions. As far as is reasonably practicable, all appliances should be kept in a good state of repair. For this reason, visual display equipment should be regularly checked for damage. Any appliance which is consequently found to be faulty or potentially dangerous should, where possible, be immediately isolated from the electrical supply and reported to a supervisor.

It is required by law that employees using VDUs should have regular breaks. (9) ____ In both cases supervisors are responsible for ensuring that these breaks are observed. The company provides word processors which have been specially selected to provide a safe system of work and every effort has been made to ensure that they have been ergonomically designed. (10) ____ This may be due to individual physical characteristics of the operator rather than the machine itself. In such cases, the company is obliged to take every action to improve the situation.

All employees are expected to notify their manager about any discomfort experienced whilst using a word processor. (11) ____Where entries refer to eyesight, display screen users are entitled, upon request, to a free eye test, the cost to be met by the company. If a user is said by his/her optician to require frequent eye tests, the employer should meet the costs of all necessary tests. (12) ____ Operators are otherwise entitled to one free eye test every twelve months unless there are exceptional medical circumstances which have arisen during the period between examinations.

The development of office networks has resulted in modular configurations, comprising a number of interchangeable computers which may be easily moved around. (13) ____ Moreover, employees should take care to ensure that no undue strain is caused through lifting in the wrong way.

It is the responsibility of all employees to report accidents. (14) ____ This may help prevent a more serious incident from happening in the future.

Read the health and safety guidelines. Choose the best sentence from a–h to fill in each gap. For each gap, mark one letter a–g. Do not mark any letter more than once.

a. Any such complaints should be recorded in the company's Health and Safety log book.

b. A supervisor should be notified immediately of all occurrences, however minor, so that appropriate action can be taken.

c. These should be taken regardless of whether they follow a period of intense or occasional use.

d. Attention is drawn to the possible dangers in seeking to carry too heavy a load.

e. However, in some cases, the operation of such equipment can have an adverse effect.

f. Hazards such as these must be reported immediately to the manager or any other person authorised to act on his or her behalf.

g. This provision is restricted to situations where the need arises because of the employee's work.

Think of a successful domestic brand in your country. Write a proposal on how the brand could be globalised.

Part III   Business knowledge and translation

 Briefly define the following underlined business terms in English and translate each term into Chinese.

1. The team wants to keep the crowdsourcing as part of its future projects, ideas and requests for which range across the U.K.
   Definition: _____
   Translation: _____

2. Already, the outsourcing of human resources is becoming an increasingly common trend.
   Definition: _____
   Translation: _____

3. Corporate Social Responsibility is a new business mentality in postindustrial society.
   Definition: _____
   Translation: _____

4. IPO restart is inevitable—it has not been any suspense.
   Definition: _____
   Translation: _____

5. Moreover, shareholders nowadays desire and respond to dividends.
   Definition: _____
   Translation: _____

Translate the following passage into English.

　　股票价格在去年年底时还比较稳定。但就在圣诞节后，价格开始浮动。在 2 月底到达最低谷后，股票价格开始反弹。然而，即使之后有几次小幅上升，股票价格仍然一再跌落，其主要原因在于投资者开始抛售股票。